All the best
Jay Bernard
2005

Memories are Made
of This...

by

Jay Bernard

authorHOUSE™

1663 LIBERTY DRIVE, SUITE 200
BLOOMINGTON, INDIANA 47403
(800) 839-8640
WWW.AUTHORHOUSE.COM

First published by AuthorHouse 11/10/04

ISBN: 1-4208-0069-8 (sc)
ISBN: 1-4208-0070-1 (dj)

Printed in the United States of America
Bloomington, Indiana

This book is printed on acid-free paper.

TABLE OF CONTENTS

PREFACE

Memories, is a collection of short stories based on the life of a farm family as it interacted and evolved in the 1940's and 50's. Although some stories are sad in nature, most are humorous.

Most stories have a factual base. Indeed, many are derived from a combination of events afforded from a far less complicated lifestyle. *Memories*, invites the reader to take a leisurely stroll along the paths offered by a less troubled age when expectations were often limited to simple wants or desires and easier joys.

Undemanding enjoyment also meant a far more accessible form of happiness when family ties were still very high on the list of values of the people of the West. The hurry-scurry of daily jobs and high technical lifestyle didn't come into play in those days. In the short life span of the average adult, we have watched the first satellite being launched into outer-space, saw man walking on the moon, space travel becoming common place and computers taking a prominent place in our life. But our grand parents struggled with their day to day existence and strove toward happiness amid what we would consider today as the very basics of life's fiber.

Within *Memories*, the reader is offered the opportunity to sit back, relax and take a trip into the past. To some, this will be a nostalgic journey, while others will gain a new experience. Whatever the case, only enjoyment awaits the reader within its pages.

THE EARLY DAYS

Scarlet fever was running rampant through the neighbourhood and had now entered their household. Although the disease could cause death or long term illness, in this case, the disease would pass and leave the infant alive. The mother, too, would escape the ominous call of the Angel of Death.

As the child grew, he discovered animals. Indeed, it seemed that any and every animal was merely alive to become one of his pets. The first pets arrived shortly after his first birthday in the form of two Scotch Collie pups, twins. The two little fellows were grey and white and the three grew close and matured together, caring deeply for each other and sharing as many hours of the day as possible.

Then came the more irregular pets – first, the ducks became amusing. He learned that by removing duck eggs from their nest, just prior to the emergence of the ducklings, it would ensure that the first thing the little fellows would see upon their entry into the world would be him. They would adopt the surrogate mother immediately and follow wherever he led.

Perhaps the most unusual pets of all were the piglets. Black and white, the two piglets had been petted and pampered by the child and his older brother until they followed them around the farm yard like puppy dogs.

One problem occurred, however, as the piglets matured and grew into adulthood. The two boys had chosen their pets but the pigs became very large sows and did not seem to agree with the choice. The sow

1

chosen by the older brother followed the younger boy everywhere and the second chose to follow the older. How frustrating it was. What could be done? The two boys attempted to change the minds of the pigs to no avail. In the end there was only one possible avenue to pursue. They traded pigs!

Many times the boys had turned the common livestock into pets but, as the animals grew into adults, they would forget their human counter parts and return to their normal existence. This was not the case with pigs. Having grown into adults and, after all, being farm animals, the day arrived when they would bear little piglets of their own.

It seemed that this development would spell the end of the relationship between the boys and their piggy pals, as the sows became mean and protective of their offspring. No more would the little boy enjoy rides around the farmyard on the back of his friend. Then, one afternoon, his mother searched for him, frantically calling his name – no answer was heard. On the chance that her son may have ventured to the granaries where the sows were housed with their piglets, panic set in. As she approached, she worried that he may have crawled in with one of the new families and had been harmed. In part, her fears were well founded. Sure enough, there he was, curled up peacefully and sleeping amid the porgy's family, his head resting on the huge sow while calmly holding one of the piglets in his arms.

Although the sows had become outwardly mean, there was no doubt that his porky pal had remembered the old days. Or, perhaps, it was merely her motherly instincts that were surfacing.

TWINS

The two puppies were identical. His father had returned home with the two bundles of grey and white fur. How lucky could one little boy be? Two puppies – and they were just for him.

At one year of age, of course, the boy was far too young to understand what was happening. But he could understand that everyone was excited. The atmosphere was charged with electricity and sparks seemed to jump from person to person. And what was the very first thing the two fur balls did? Why run right toward the baby and lick his face thoroughly. The little fellow felt a certain kinship with the puppies and giggled, enjoying their attention.

As the months rolled on to become years, the three grew closer and closer until it was impossible to find one dog or the boy alone. They ran, at all times, and always as a group. The little boy laughed happily and both pups bounded alongside, barking. They were the best of friends.

However, the closeness between the lad and his hairy friends, on occasion, caused jealousy and could create a situation where the two dogs were pitted against one another. On one of these occasions, when the boy was three years old, while playing with the dogs on the step of the little house, he began to cry. No one knew what started the crying, but it was the loudest crying the dogs had ever heard.

Each dog blamed the other for the pain he was suffering. They promptly turned on each other, feeling both jealous and protective. Snarling, fangs bared, a fight ensued.

As the summer days shortened and the crispness of fall began, the disaster on the step was forgotten. Once again, the family trusted the child alone with his two friends. The entire incident had been a misunderstanding and, the parents realized, neither dog had threatened to harm their son. They were attempting to offer protection. So the three buddies resumed their exploration of the land and trees surrounding the house and out buildings of the farm.

But, as if two dogs were not enough of a problem, the boy's father decided to augment the farm income by starting a trap line for weasels and hunting coyotes for their pelts. He returned from town one afternoon with greyhounds and a Russian Wolf Hound. Now, instead of two, there were seven dogs on the farm, all running free, their lives unencumbered by leash or pen.

At most times there wasn't any problem. However, the proximity of the animals led to snarling and biting. A great deal of jealousy roamed among the dogs and it seemed the only time the hounds ventured forth in a united effort, was when they were chasing a coyote. Quite naturally, the Collies, being protective of their property reacted to the newcomers and were often blamed for the disturbances.

As the weeks and seasons passed, rapidly turning into years, problems continued with the dogs. While returning home with team and hay wagon, the hounds and Collies began to growl and fight in a flooded creek.

Not daring to jump from the hay rack and land among the snarling animals, the boy watched as his oldest brother shouted, in a vain attempt to gain the attention of the angry beasts. Nothing seemed to work. He could not distract the animals as the struggle continued to intensify.

He decided to end the battle using the only method he felt would possibly be effective. He picked up a three tined pitch fork and threw it amongst the splashing, growling animals, attempting to distract them from their purpose. It seemed to work! A loud yelp was heard by the boys on the rack and the dogs dispersed. Only something seemed very wrong.

One of the Collie twins lay in the water. He moved ever so little, and then fell back. Something must be done or the dog would drown.

The eldest brother jumped into the swirling water of the creek and picked up the small grey dog. As quickly as possible, he returned to the hay rack and laid the dog on the floor.

"Don't worry", he told his little brother, "We'll fix him."

They carried the pup to the barn and began to nurse him and bandage his wounds. Surely he would recover!

As evening crept upon them, the family returned to the house and made their way to bed. The youngest boy continued to worry about his friend but the older members of the family assured him that everything, which could be done for the dog, had been done. The night would unravel the story. If the dog lived until morning, the worst would be over.

Throughout the long spring night the child remained in his bed, sleeping a troubled sleep. When morning came, he crawled out of bed with the first rays of dawn, awakened his older brother and headed for the barn hoping to see the Collie up and moving around.

They opened the door and entered. But there was no movement in the barn. There had been twin dogs, but now there was one.

Jay Bernard

MARY

Anyone questioning the hardiness of farm girls of the twenties and thirties had never met Mary.

When Mary arrived at her new place of employment she was still in her teens and relatively inexperienced but, with patience on the part of her instructor and dedication on her part, she quickly learned and developed the skills necessary to become one of the best housekeepers in the area. She carried out her duties with love and dedication and assisted with the care of the children. During the time she stayed with her new found family it grew from one boy until it was composed of two boys and a girl. The three adults and the three children were then living in a small, two-story house with one room on each floor.

Mary loved the children and treated them as if they were her brothers and sisters, loving them and caring for them day in and day out.

Although life was hard with no electricity or running water, she adapted and made this new environment her home. But then the Great Depression came, which changed the lives of everyone in the entire country. Those who had been successful previously, suddenly, found themselves short of clothing, money, or, in some cases, adequate food. Times were difficult, but thanks to hard work and what their neighbours called a "green thumb" the little family never went without food, although often the fare was quite simple. It was, in fact, not unusual to eat potatoes and other vegetables without any

7

other trimmings which would have been considered as 'frivolous' at the time. And with the loss, a decision had to be made about Mary.

As the future of the family became more and more questionable, the time finally arrived when it had obviously become necessary to inform the young maid that it was no longer possible to continue the payment of her salary. Having grown quite attached to the children and their parents, Mary chose to remain in their home, even though she could not be paid for her services.

Life settled down to some extent.

The young lady settled in, quite content to carry on the life to which she had become accustomed. She seemed to thrive on the arrangement of no longer functioning in the role of an employee. Indeed, she appeared to relish her new position as a part of the family and blossomed with the experience.

Years after the birth of their third child, a fourth child arrived. And this one, Mary decided, would be special. Mary loved caring for the new born and treated the little boy as if he were her own. Actually, anything that posed a threat to any of her children was in great jeopardy.

On one occasion, the family's two Collies began to fight, as each thought the other was hurting the child. Without hesitation, Mary rushed in between the two snarling animals and plucked the child from harm's way and brought him to safety within the house; but not before her momentum sent her sprawling backwards over an apple box child and all.

On another, an angry rooster decided the little boy must be taught a lesson and, wings dragging on the ground, attempted to flog the lad. Mary jumped to the rescue. Without hesitation, she leaped into action; the bird lost the battle and became dinner. No one or nothing fooled around with the great protector.

Arriving home from their shopping excursion to the nearest town late one afternoon, the family was shocked to see a pool of fresh blood in the lane. After further investigation, it was impossible to tell whether it was human blood or that of an animal and, of course, the very worst scenario leapt to mind. Rushing into the house they were pleased to find everyone safe, except for one of the largest of the turkey gobblers, which they had been raising to sell at Christmas. It was in the process of being cleaned and prepared for the oven. It seems that it had angered Mary by attempting to attack one of the children and she had struck it with a broom that she happened to be holding.

One thing was certain; her protective measures always seemed to alter the dinner menu.

Time continued to pass and the family moved from the farm to one town and then another but, Mary moved with them and remained part of the family for many years hence. She, in fact, remained a family member for life, although she was to leave what had become her family, when she reached the later years of her life. This time, she was to be on her own permanently.

Indeed, by the time she moved out to lead a life of her own, she had been with her adopted family well over thirty years and was in excess of fifty years of age. In many ways, the children of the family were members of Mary's family as much as she had been a part of theirs.

Jay Bernard

HOUNDS

They appeared out of nowhere.

One day the farm was quiet and serene and the next there were barking dogs everywhere! They did not belong. But there they were. Everything had changed.

The hounds, Greyhounds, had been purchased to help supplement the income of the family. It was hoped that the dogs could bring down more coyotes than normal and, therefore, result in a larger income. The youngest son, however, doubted if they would even earn their keep. They were nothing but a problem.

There were six Greyhounds and one Russian wolfhound. Each had its own personality and each operated on a different plane of intelligence when it came to interaction between the dogs and their owners. In fact, all seemed rather slow mentally.

Bismarck had a very long nose with the head slightly higher than the eyes. Nor was "Old Bis" coloured in the same manner as the others. He was brown while the remainder of the pack were black and white or even a bluish hue.

Bismarck was a relatively intelligent animal compared to the others, who loved to scout, lay in ambush or engage humans in mock attack. He would lay waiting in a ditch or obscured in the reeds along the lane, until someone passed his way and then, dart forward and grab the wrist of the unsuspecting dupe in his jaws. He had made his capture, therefore, there was little risk of injury since the old dog would never close his jaws. Indeed, the jaws closed only hard enough to leave a slight imprint of the canine teeth on the unsuspecting subject's wrists.

For those who were not aware of the dog's habits, this could be a devastating experience, but the family found him playful and amusing, if not actually loveable.

As for the rest of the pack, they were individuals too. Two were stereotype Greyhounds, white in colour with black patches on their bodies; although they were friendly, neither seemed to be very smart. Indeed when the hounds tangled with a porcupine, it was inevitable that these two would be the dogs with the highest number of quills in their mouths; quills, which could only be extracted with a pair of pliers and a great deal of pain and howling. The wailing of the hounds and the extreme energy required both to control the dog and to extract the hurtful darts made the chore distasteful.

Then there was the Russian wolfhound, Old Ruff. He was adequately named, as he was large, had long hair and exhibited rough physical features. In personality, however, he was anything but rough. His nature, with humans was rather sublime and he tolerated children to the extreme. Indeed, children could jump on him, pull his fur or subject him to any form of torture; the old dog would never, growl, bark or react. With coyotes, it was a different story as he would willingly do his job when the demand was placed upon him.

Another individual of the pack, Blue, probably demonstrated the highest degree of intelligence of the entire group. Although the main pack would follow a coyote's every move without thought, Blue was less distracted. He seemed to avail himself of a degree of cleverness close to that of his quarry and would, in many cases, save the beast from realizing its flight to freedom. Other animals would jump about at the smell of the coyote and seem certain that, because the spoor was evident, the coyote was present. Blue on the other hand, depended on his astuteness and sight and was seldom fooled.

But the hounds retained their value, only as long as there was a sufficient bounty on coyotes or when the pelts retained adequate value.

Finally it happened. The free meals had come to an end, coyote pelts were worth little and the bounty on coyotes had become inadequate or non existent. There was no alternative but to free the family of the burden.

For several months, an attempt was made to offer the hounds to good homes, free, but finally there was no hope left. The hounds must be removed from the farm.

One morning, as the sun rose, father and my two older brothers left the small house and made their way over the hill and off toward the brush by the creek. The hounds were on leashes and the decision had been made. Surely there was no other answer, as the family had tried all other alternatives.

The animals just seemed to disappear.

Jay Bernard

COYOTE! COYOTE!

Growing up on the prairies in the mid to late nineteen forties was quite different from the experiences of children in the sixties or later. Indeed, the "Great Depression" was fresh in the memories of everyone and, in many cases; families were still attempting to rebuild their lives and focus on what appeared to be a more positive future. Many, in fact, were still making an effort to recoup the losses they had suffered during the thirties.

Farm families were probably hit hardest during this period of time as many had lost their livestock, their machinery or even their land. One family was one of these, yet they were slightly more fortunate than some. They had managed to keep their land; a quarter section, during that period in history which had brought about the demise of so many.

To make ends meet, farming simply wasn't enough. With most of the livestock gone, the crops raised on a quarter section of land could barely supply the bare necessities of an average family and definitely would not allow for any monetary gains. Therefore, other sources of income had to be found. In the case of this family, this meant running a trap line for weasels, coyotes or any other furry creatures that were unfortunate enough to be caught. Prices were high for the time, with a good quality weasel pelt bringing as much as fifteen or seventeen dollars.

Every day, the father traveled along his line, removing carcasses, replacing bait and resetting traps. Every night, the day's catch was skinned. This in itself was an experience. The smaller animals, especially the weasels, were brought into the house and skinned on the kitchen floor, the only room on the main floor of a little two-story home. Most often, the deed was accomplished while sitting in front of the coal stove which heated the dwelling. If everything went well, at the end of an evening they would find themselves a few pelts richer. But weasels are members of the skunk family and carry a similar aroma. One slip of the knife and the house would reek through the night. In many cases, the pungent reminder still hung in the air at breakfast the next morning.

In addition to the trap line, it was found necessary to hunt coyotes using a pack of Greyhounds and a half Russian wolfhound.

While attempting to locate a coyote, the hounds were carried in the back of a 1928 Chevy four-door sedan, from which the back seat had been removed. Upon sighting the prey, the dogs were set free to run it down. It sounds so simple and one would suppose that quite an inequality exists with six or seven large dogs chasing one poor little coyote, but the intelligence and cunning of the wild dog should never be underestimated.

Compared to a coyote who must earn its living with its wiles, domestic dogs are completely out-classed. Finding a hay stack, the coyote will calmly run up the closest side, lie on top of it and watch the dogs approach. Upon reaching the stack, the hounds would set up a terrible ruckus, barking and whining while jumping aimlessly at the near side of the stack, attempting to reach their prey. Meanwhile, Mr. Coyote will look down on them, fully aware he is far beyond their reach.

Let a man approach, however, the coyote instantly recognizes the danger and calmly moves to the back of the hay stack, jumps down and runs off across the field toward the nearest cover. The hounds, on the other hand, continue to jump and bark, totally unaware that the source of their interest has long since departed. Stupidity rules until their master arrives and, forcefully, takes them under his control and points them on the trail of the coyote. Only now, do they realize the error of their ways and the chase resumes.

With the hounds closing in on their target, and if no cover exists, the coyote will head as rapidly as possible for a fence line. Not much cover along a wire fence line, right? Fence posts are placed ten or fifteen feet apart with three strands of barbed wire between them.

Wrong! The coyote instinctively knows the hounds are faster and possess more stamina than he, so he trots along, switching sides of the fence as he goes. Each time the quarry switches sides, a traffic jamb of hounds is a certainty. They switch sides of the fence each time their victim does, bumping into each other or straining to get under the bottom wire as they go. Only when the fence ends will the hounds manage to corner their game.

Coyotes are amazing creatures in many ways, and exhibit a great deal of flair when attempting to snatch a free lunch from a farmer's stock. Inevitably, they will choose the most vulnerable.

Many farmers chose to build outdoor perches for turkeys. Shortly after dawn, a coyote may appear and calmly turn in circles beneath the perches. The turkeys, being inquisitive by nature begin to watch. Swaying gently to follow the coyote's circle, they become dizzy, fall, and became dinner as soon as they touch the ground.

And to suggest that wild animals, in general, and coyotes especially, do not communicate readily is a great farce. Time and again, communication has been proven.

The first day, one lone coyote may come into the yard and steal away with a turkey. The following day he will bring his mate, and the following day the entire family will come to dinner.

Coyote pelts became quite worthless in the early fifties, as a result hunting came to an end. Instead, many farmers viewed coyotes as a threat to their livestock, especially in the spring, when the cattle were calving. Communities organized what was known as "Coyote Drives" which were totally inhumane and had no valid purpose. Where would they drive the poor animals? To their deaths!

A group of hunters would spread out, make a great deal of noise and moving forward, steadily close the circle of men converging on a predetermined clump of brush. It was hoped every animal in the area would be chased out of reach before the advancing men and that they would be able to seek shelter. Once on target, the men would come through the brush from one side, flushing out anything in their path, while the rest would wait for the exiting animals and calmly shoot the coyotes in a cold blood. This was called a "Sunday sport".

Fortunately, farmers, in most cases, have realized that coyotes are not the great threat to livestock they once thought; especially if there is enough natural prey. Coyotes would certainly prefer mice, gophers and the odd wild bird to challenging the farmer's rifle. Many a pair would come within thirty feet of a farm well; lie down beside the machinery and watch the family moving about carrying on their daily activities as barnyard hens wandered aimlessly on the grass nearby.

Yes, respect the coyote and its intelligence. In spite of the efforts of man, with his supposedly superior brain, they have managed to exist and now nearly co-exist with human population, living on the prairies, in the mountains and even in the brushed area of Hollywood, California.

Here's to the Coyote!

SCHOOL DAYS

School days in the nineteen forties and fifties were a carefree time for students. They did not have all the games, copying equipment and fancy paraphernalia of today but the children 'learned'.

Many students started school at age seven or eight due to the difficulty of traveling three or more miles to school. Indeed, summer or winter meant travel by car, by horseback, by tractor or even on foot. Without school buses it was difficult.

Spring and fall seasons were especially troublesome for most of the families as it was busy on the farm. On many occasions, students as young as grade five and six were absent from school during these busy times. In fact, it was not unusual for eight year olds to be driving what seemed at that time, a very large truck and hauling grain.

Arriving at the old school house to begin education and a new decade, many may recall the much dreaded arrival.

Held firmly in tow by two older brothers, both of whom were out of school with advanced educations, grade nine and ten, one new student made his way over rutted roads in an old car. It was one of the most frightening experiences of many a young life.

As they entered the school yard, they could hear the clamour of children playing, seemingly happy to see one another again after a long summer. They were behind the school house playing softball and having a joyous time. Soon the new boy recognized one. No! Two, then three and four and so on; for Heavens sake, these children

19

were mostly cousins! Now this was a whole different ball game. One that he could play!

Upon sighting him, several cousins, who knew he could play the game as well as most children, extended the invitation to take part. It was great! Some of the bigger boys, most often grade nines, hit the ball a long way. There seemed to be a contest at hand as they attempted to hit the ball over the roof of the old horse barn.

But all good things must come to an end and the day soon took a turn for the worse. The teacher disappeared, reappearing momentarily on the steps of the old school, ringing a hand held bell. He had never heard a bell ring in such a manner and had no idea what the response was to be but, as the other children headed reluctantly toward the door of the school, he followed their lead. The first day of instruction was about to begin!

The teacher, a very pleasant lady in her mid twenties, looked in his direction and said, "Benny, would you please sit at this table?"

Looking around, Ben realized that all the younger children, whom he later learned were in grades one and two, were sitting on small chairs at long, low tables. The one the teacher indicated seemed to be home to about four other children, two were his cousins. Older cousins in their second year of school were seated at a second table not far away.

Frightened but determined to do his best and mind the teacher, as he had been cautioned before leaving home, he sat at the indicated table, intent on what the teacher might do next.

She turned her attention to his table, smiled and said, "Here are some scribblers and pencils. Everyone write your name on the front page and the alphabet on the next".

Although often home schooled, for these children education varied. One stared off into space and played with her pencil and finally began to draw a stick figure. It was in the appropriate section, under name so it could be guessed it was her way of showing ownership. Some carefully printed their names in the proper area, opened the cover and began their alphabet. Ben tried to follow their example.

Returning to check their work, the teacher, looked at the girl's drawing. "Very good," she said. "Is this you?"

Looking at the books Ben's cousins, she showed a great deal of satisfaction at their printed names and alphabets. "Good work!" she said, "Now can you write your numbers from one through ten?"

They began to move their pencils on their papers once again.

Ben was next. Oh, how he hoped for the teacher's approval. But when she looked at the paper, she seemed shocked.

"Why, Benny," she said. "You've written your name, not printed it."

Ben was destroyed. He had failed to follow instructions and please the teacher. And he had promised faithfully to do his best before leaving home that morning. Now, first time she asked him to do something he had failed. How would he ever make this up to her?

It took little time for the question to be answered. The teacher turned to Ben and asked him to pick up his supplies and move to another table. He was embarrassed. He was disheartened! How could he ever please this woman? Or would she leave him alone and never make a request of him again?

As the year went on, Ben was asked many times how he was enjoying school. Inevitably, he would reply, "Fine." But when asked what grade he was in he avoided the question while his parents answered, "Oh, Benny's in grade one."

However, he knew he had been moved from the grade one table and doomed to failure. Perhaps next year he would be able to say he was in grade one but, for this year, it seemed he had been forgotten.

With the passing months, Ben soon learned to look forward to Fridays which featured the equivalent of physical education class. During the winter months, one typical activity was held outside and usually consisted of games of Fox and Goose, building snow forts and snow men or having snowball fights.

At the beginning of June, however, activities began in a competitive vein. Students were loaded into a farmer's truck and delivered to the next school where the entire group of boys played a baseball game with their hosts.

With the end of the school year the annual picnic came. In reality, it was a picnic with lunch and ice cream, a rare commodity. But at the same time, it was little more than a modified track meet where everyone participated and won prizes. Events began with the younger children and finally ended when the mothers, in their dresses, raced.

At the end of the picnic, the moment Ben had been dreading arrived. Report cards were handed out! His family would learn of his disgrace at last! It could no longer be hidden.

The teacher handed Ben his report card and he opened it slowly, afraid to hand it to his parents. It read, "Benny has been promoted to grade three."

Grade three!

A year's worth of worry had been for nothing. He had been in grade one for minutes. What appeared as being banned had been an instant promotion. He had tried his best and completed his work diligently but he had missed something. What was missed, however, was anything but what had been expected.

He had missed grade one!

SURPRISE
AT SUNRISE

The night exploded. Noises rang out everywhere! Dogs barked, growled, quieted and renewed the excitement.

Perhaps it was a neighbour's cat straying onto the property again. They could only hope. There was always a concern about cats molesting the birds that dwelled in the bird houses scattered around the yard. Every time one came near, the dogs would tree it and bark. It was the signal for someone to awaken and venture into the yard and take care of the troublesome visitor.

Expecting feline guests, the boys and their father leapt from their beds, pulled on clothing and dashed outdoors, grabbing a shotgun and a twenty two rifle as they passed the door. They would dispose of this problem in short order.

Search as they may, they could not discover the whereabouts of the interloper. It was strange. Normally, the dogs would be looking up a tree and barking but, this time, they were confused. They didn't go near the trees or bushes that surrounded the house. Instead, they searched near the chicken house, dashing to and fro and becoming more excited with the passing minutes.

Surely they were mistaken. Perhaps a coyote had strayed near the chicken coop and was frightened away by the hounds. It was impossible for one of the wild dogs to gain entry to the enclosure where the chickens were housed so, most certainly, the visitor had departed.

More minutes passed before the older man suggested the dogs may have given a false alarm. There were no cats to be found and nothing could manage to gain entry to the chickens.

The father looked slowly up another tree, turned to his sons and said, "I guess there's nothing we can do here boys. Let's hit the sack. Morning comes early and there's lots of work to be done tomorrow."

Tiredly, the boys moved across the front yard and into the house, returning, gratefully, to their beds. They were content to follow their father's instructions, return to dreamland and grab as much sleep as possible before they would be called for morning chores. Their heads barely touched the pillows before their eyes shut and they drifted off.

The night passed quickly. It seemed they had only returned to their beds when the morning arrived and the alarm clock rudely awakened them. Climbing out of bed, they pulled on their clothes and headed out into the early summer sunlight. Bruce would get the cows from the pasture, Charles would busy himself feeding the pigs and the younger son followed his father about, as usual. They moved at random, here and there around the yard, opening gates, feeding the hounds and finally, moving toward the hen house to release the fowl for another day.

On approaching the door, something seemed unusually. Most mornings, hens were singing and pecking at the inside of the door, waiting to be released. But this morning everything was quiet.

The boys watched anxiously, as their father opened the door to the chicken coop. He moved about normally and displayed no sign of the anxiety he felt. But something seemed badly wrong. The man opened the hen house door and froze. Froze in his tracks! Barely breathing, he stood quietly, motionless, no muscle moving. The silence was unnerving.

Then the boy saw it! Walking nonchalantly through his father's legs, he caught the sight and smell of a skunk. It was not in a hurry but merely ambled out through the door way and started on its way.

As it moved three or four meters past the frozen farmer, the skunk stopped, turned, looked over his shoulder at the motionless man for a moment and then resumed its slow departure.

In a moment, Bruce came around the corner of the building, loading a rifle as he came. But the skunk seemed to have disappeared under an abandoned outhouse.

Farmers knew that once a skunk has been in the henhouse, it will return. So the problem had to be handled, and handled now.

With help from his brothers and father, the corner of the old structure was raised. Cautiously, Bruce bent to look underneath, prepared to send the skunk to a better world. But just as he aimed the rifle and readied himself to squeeze the trigger he let out a yelp.

Bruce was noted for his snap shooting. But, this time, he had been up against a rival who was even quicker on the trigger.

TAILLESS PORKERS

He'd been warned before, perhaps a hundred times. He wouldn't listen to reason. What could they do?

As Ben saw them coming, he could hear his father's words ring in his ears.

"Fix your pens Wilf. Keep your pigs at home, they're ruining our garden."

But Wilf hadn't listened. Here they came again! Pigs were everywhere. Wilf wasn't the most energetic person in the world it seemed. In fact, he was much disorganized and, as a result, he simply never got around to making repairs to his pig pens. He didn't mind, though, as his animals never stayed home to bother him or mess up his yard when they did escape. Inevitably, they decided to trek to some neighbour's house to explore new territory.

Ben called to his father, "Dad, Wilf's pigs are out again!"

The door to the house opened and out came the whole family, Dad, Mom, two older brothers and, finally, Ben's sister. They were on the run, hoping to cut off the intruders before they spread throughout the yard and damaged everything in sight. As the chase began the pigs split and headed in a variety of directions, running here and there through the rows of carriganas, in and out through the Russian Poplars and around buildings. The only place they didn't run was into their pens.

Ben shouted, whistled and waived his arms and one of the big sows began to run. She headed straight along the side of the hen house. Just as she reached the corner, disaster struck; another large sow came from the opposite direction, Mary, in hot pursuit. Well, that was it; the two sows joined forces and headed off across the yard. The chase would start over.

Mary moved toward the two sows, broom in hand, prepared to do anything necessary.

"Get those animals out of there," she shouted as she took after the pigs with her broom swinging.

Ben felt just a little sorry for the poor pigs. They didn't know who they were dealing with. In fact, Mary was one of the most violent women he knew, when it came to chasing animals.

Mary took another wild swing with the broom, slapping it broad side across the flanks of the nearest pig and hurrying it along. The old sow gave a squeal and jumped forward.

Although the family had forgotten about the family dog, Buck, he had decided to get into the action without invitation and charged the closest pig. It ran for the fence with Buck right behind. Just as the pig's snout started under the lowest strand of barbed wire, Buck grabbed its tail in his mouth and planted his feet firmly. The pig had decided to go home and nothing, certainly not a weight on her tail, was going to stop her.

Under the fence went the pig but Buck remained steadfast on his side. The pig's tail had come off! There sat the old dog, a confused look on his face, with the pig's tail dangling from his mouth.

Buck thought his action plan was sound. The pig had not stayed around to question his intent but, feeling an excruciating pain from behind, headed down the driveway and straight for home. If it worked once, why not try it again?

The dog dropped the tail from his mouth and looked for the closest pig. As hard as it was to believe, he chased the next one toward the same area of fence and followed his plan. Under the fence went the pig and Buck sat with a tail in his mouth. Once again the pig continued on its way, running until reaching the safety of its own pen.

When the family noticed what was happening they stopped chasing animals to laugh. It was just as well. Buck had no need for help. The former herders watched and laughed as the dog chased one animal after another under the fence, removing its tail as it went. He continued until the entire group of interlopers had been challenged and sent back in the direction from which they had first appeared.

The next day, Ben and his eldest brother, Charles, paid Wilf, a visit. As it was early in the morning, he was found in his barn, milking cows.

"How's it goin', Wilf?" asked Charles.

Wilf looked up from the milking stool on which he was sitting and said, "Just fine, Chuck. How's everything with you?"

The small talk continued for a short time before Wilf got around to a topic of concern.

"You know, I think there's something wrong with my pigs," he said. "Just about every one of them had its tail drop off. Do you think something's wrong? Maybe they're missing something in their diet and eating each others tails. What do you think, Chuck?"

The brothers began to laugh, and told their story of "Why the pigs had no tails."

Although Wilf did not seem very amused, neither was he angry. He smiled blandly as he picked up a hammer. Calmly, he strolled across the yard, toward the pig pens and began to hammer nails to repair the pig pens.

SWIMMIN'
AIN'T POSSIBLE!

Someone should have told her. But they had not! And now, she was beside herself with fear!

It began some days earlier, when the farmer's wife had set duck eggs under the hen. There weren't enough prospective mothers among the duck population so a hen would have to do. The eggs would still be incubated and would soon be hatched into a clutch of young ducklings.

Upon hatching the hen had accepted the ducklings as her own. But she was too low on the intelligence scale to recognize them as ducklings. To her, they were her babies.

She strutted, proudly, through the yard, her wards following closely behind. She didn't notice that they "quacked" rather than "cheeped". Nor did she notice that they slurped their food, never pecked and could not be taught how to scratch. To her their actions were all totally meaningless. They did; however, seem to recognize her clucks when she called them or her warnings as they strayed too far away. Indeed, they followed her every instruction as would any chick in the hen yard.

It took several days for the problem to finally surface. Previously, the hen led her offspring around the yard, looking for food or water and snuggling them under her wings for protection, as they slept.

All went well. It was a normal, happy family. That is until the hen led her charges farther away from the hen house than usual. On that fateful day, they wandered through the wood, searching here and there for bugs or seeds from wild plants to satisfy their appetites for both food and adventure.

As they cleared the wooded area, a small slough lay before them. Without hesitation, the young ducklings, gleefully, entered the water and began to paddle about. Their adopted mother was beside herself with fear. What were her offspring trying to do? Did they not realize that water was dangerous? Their feathers would soon become water logged! They would sink and drown!

Call to them as she would, the youngsters ignored their mother and continued to enjoy themselves in the waters of the slough.

This caused further concern on the part of the hen. She must get her babies out of the water before something happened to them. They must return to safety.

Disregarding her own safety and overcoming her fears, the hen waded into the water. But it was no use. She was still unable to reach them. They had paddled into deeper water. Cluck as she would, they ignored her frantic calls and attempts to gain their attention and, ultimately, gain control of the situation. They quacked happily and continued to paddle about.

Still deeper, the hen waded into the slough, until she felt the cool water lapping softly against her breast. Her feathers became wet as she ventured into ever deepening water. She had to extend her body and stand on the tips of her toes to keep her balance. The water lifted her completely off the bottom and threatened to carry her away. Still the ducklings ignored her pleas for their return to the safety of the shore.

Then it happened! She had ventured too deep into the slough! The water lifted her from the bottom and she was carried away, away from the shore, toward her babies. She must escape! She could not allow herself to drown!

Frantically, she kicked her feet in an attempt to escape the ominous threat of the water and reach the shore! To her surprise, it worked! She began to move into shallow water until she could touch bottom.

As the farmer watched, he expected the hen to wade out of the water and dry herself on shore. But, to his surprise, she did not wade out.

Instead, she began to move back into deeper water. She began to kick her feet wildly, then in a more controlled manner; indeed, she had managed to turn her body in the water and had gained a controlled rhythm to her strokes. She was swimming!

This was impossible! Hens cannot swim! Their feathers become water logged. They sink. And they drown! It was as simple as that.

Not in this case, however. The hen paddled out to her adopted babies and paddled around with them, until the entire family returned to the shore and began to walk through the woods toward the hen house.

Although it is impossible for chickens to swim, this hen had accomplished the impossible. She not only learned to swim, but she led her offspring to the slough to enjoy their swim on a daily basis.

Yes someone should have told her she had ducklings. Or at very least advised her that hens CAN NOT SWIM!

Jay Bernard

THE AUCTION

Snow lay in tiny mounds, where once great drifts had been piled by the winter's wind. Rivulets wandered between the mounds, joining and heading downhill toward the creek. It was spring! April! The day the family would find their lives changed forever.

The farmer's eldest son, Charles, had been at auction school and had returned days earlier, to help arrange machinery and other items in neat rows to catch the eye of potential buyers. The machinery was parked in the last row. It would be sold last so the crowd would remain throughout the day and bid on other items. This could even result in higher prices. Heaven only knew; the family needed as much money as they could possibly raise; if they were to make a fresh start in their new home.

Farmers had traveled miles down gravel roads to be there and the result should be a success. But, as the farmer often said, "The proof is in the pudding," and the outcome depended solely on need. If the need for his equipment was not forthcoming, the family may come up short of their financial goal and find themselves in even worse trouble.

They had fought through the Depression and, for many years, farmed the hilly land, waiting out the droughts and hail storms and tolerating poor growing conditions which seemed to never end. Regardless of what had been attempted, it never seemed to have a fruitful outcome. The crops were always barely large enough to be worth harvesting.

Perhaps more land was the answer. In one desperate attempt to save the farm and the family's way of life, another quarter section of land several miles away had been rented, but this had proven to create difficulties as the farm machinery was slow to move

Now, everything had come to a climax. No other choice remained but to sell the machinery and move away. In the new operation, pasture land would be leased as an addition and there were no fields to plow or plant. All they would be taking along was an old truck and their furniture. What future awaited them?

The auctioneering crew arrived early that spring morning. At ten o'clock, the activity began. The auctioneer tested his microphone, cleared his throat and began, "Alright! What am I bid for this group of shovels, boys? You can never have too many of these lying around."

A voice came from the crowd, faceless to the youth who watched the only life he had ever known begin to disappear before his very eyes; "Five bucks!"

"Five dollars bid, who'll give me six? Six! Six! Can I hear…" the auctioneer's voice droned on.

As the boy sank into thought, it seemed the voice disappeared, rapidly becoming nothing.

He could only think of the life he was about to leave. Oh, moving was exciting alright but with it came uncertainty. This simply did not seem a suitable way to celebrate his eleventh birthday. It spelled the end of life, as he had known it. All that remained was a very obscure future, a journey into the unknown.

He moved away from the auctioneer. He had not cared for the drone of the old fellow. Later on Charles had been promised a chance to take the auction stand to show what he had learned at auction school. The boy had spent many hours singing along with his big brother or attempting to learn the auction cry so he knew his bother was fast. He would return for the treat.

As he moved across the pasture between the barn and the house, the boy stopped to look at the hillside. Once again, it was a beautiful blue, coloured by thousands of crocuses that popped through every spring. How he loved to pick a bouquet of those crocuses. He waited patiently every year, until enough snow melted and the frost left the ground, allowing the dainty flowers to exhibit their resplendence.

Wandering, aimlessly, toward the crest of the small hill he was intent on his prize. It was only a tiny rise but, since they used it for sleigh riding in the winter they called it a hill. He looked down, admiringly, at the crocuses at his feet, chose one and picked it. Then he picked another, and another, until his hand was filled with the delicate blue flowers. With his mission accomplished, he straightened and began to walk toward the house.

As he neared an open window in the house, used for serving hot coffee, with his flowers, the boy wondered why he was giving things away. Why had everyone forgotten? It was, after all, his birthday. Should someone not remember? He would certainly remember this day! Sunny, pleasant but, due to the activities of the day, it was a dark day in the life of the youngster. This was definitely not the birthday gift he had hoped for.

Fighting back the tears, he handed the flowers through the opening of the window to his mother.

"The . . . they're for all of you," he stammered. "The whole hillside's blue again." Then he quickly withdrew, having difficulty maintaining his self control.

He realized this would be the very last spring, the very last day, that he would be able to pick crocuses for his mother.

As he moved toward the barnyard, he heard the auctioneer introduce his older brother. "Yessiree, gen'lemen, fresh back from auction school in the United States, he is."

Now Charles would show them! And show them he did! He was certainly exciting the crowd!

Charles was talking so fast that the crowd had come alive. They were totally mesmerized, wrapped up in the rhythm. It was as if they had been sleeping, lulled into unconsciousness by the droning voice of the old auctioneer. Now they were awake.

On toward sunset, the chilling wind increased and those die hard individuals who stood by the machinery began to take refuge here and there among the combines, tractors and tillers. They hid any place to be out of the wind and yet remain close to the auctioneer, to be within hearing range to bid on the items for which they had come.

Finally, the last of the machinery was sold and the crowd moved toward their vehicles. Within minutes, it seemed, the small farm yard was deserted. There was nothing left to do but load the last of their belongings on to the old truck and head for their new home.

With one last look over their shoulders, the family began their journey to town, and their new home. It was the end of an era but, perhaps, it could also be a beginning. Perhaps the future would not be so bleak, so ominous, so imposing, as it seemed at that moment.

WE'VE MOVED

OL' PUP

    Once there had been two dogs, twins, but now only one remained. Tragedy had removed one from the young boy's life and, as a result, he grew even closer to the remaining dog.

    He could not remember the dog not being present on the little farm. Indeed, his family had told him many times that the dog had come shortly before his first birthday so it was little wonder that he could not remember the arrival.

    For hours at a time, the two would roam the fields and gambol through the countryside.

They constantly searched for new adventures, new challenges and new discoveries. Life could not be better. Wherever the lad roamed, so too, went his companion…

Then the first disaster occurred. The Collie had run with the pack of Greyhounds and the challenge was laid and soon a massive dog fight broke out. Soon the fight was out of control and the dogs turned on one another. There was little or no sense to the struggle. It was kill or be killed. Before the fight ended, the Collie had lost half an ear, among quite a few other battle injuries.

Days passed, and the Collie's ear did not seem to improve. Indeed, it seemed to worsen steadily, until infection set in. Soon the ear emitted a distasteful odour and was obviously approaching grave condition. A careful check was made and maggots were discovered.

Sunday arrived, which usually meant that some of the cousins would drop in. When the first arrived, the disagreement over Pup's fate was reaching a climax. Should the dog be destroyed, for its own good? The youth's elder brother felt there was no alternative but the youth insisted that the dog must not be put to sleep. Itching to eliminate the problem; they entered the fray which led to a bet.

"I'll bet you five dollars that dog won't live until morning," the cousin said.

The boy had no idea whether or not there was a chance of his friend living through the afternoon let alone the night but he could not see any more harm come to him. The bet was made.

To save the dog an appeal was made to the highest court on the farm, the lad's father. Should we destroy the dog?

"No," said the Judge, "Not unless Ben agrees."

There was no agreement forthcoming from the Ben. If the animal died, it would do so of the illness, not at the hands of an executioner.

"Well," said his brother. "We'll try to do something."

With that he poured kerosene into the infected ear. It required several applications, over the next few days, to bring about the desired results. But the infection subsided and maggots began to float out of the ear.

There was no assurance that the treatment would help, but it was reapplied periodically. To the amazement of the family and the joy of the boy, the dog began to show signs of renewed energy. It had worked! The dog would live! He was gaining his strength and would soon return to normal. The bet had been won, although it was never to be paid.

Again the boy and his dog would drift, aimlessly, through the fields on pleasant summer afternoons. Both the lad and the dog seemed to obtain great pleasure from these outings. The fellowship between pet and master was intense.

Time passed rapidly and, one spring morning, the boy's father informed the family that the farm had been sold and that the machinery would soon be sold at auction. He assured his family, however, that they would enjoy the new home and surroundings. And best of all it would be closer to town and the schooling would be better. Even the house would be larger. Besides, there was a large pasture which stretched away, north from the house and it would require a great deal of exploration on the part of Ben and his dog. It proved to supply many weeks of entertainment.

At the time, Ben didn't realize what was being lost but, assured that it was "all for the best" he looked forward to the move.

Although Ben expected everything to remain the same as it had been, with the exception of surroundings, they did not. Many changes occurred. Social and family life changed. Less contact with family occurred and Ben had to adjust and find company. Again he turned to his dog.

Although the boy and his dog had always spent a great deal of time together, their relationship had changed to the point that the boy relied on the dog for everything. He could do nothing without his pal. Indeed, the dog walked to the very limit of the town each day, as the boy headed off to school, before being sent home. And as if he had a built in clock, the little pal returned, each afternoon, as the boy returned home, sitting and waiting for his arrival.

As the months passed, the boy's father found it necessary to hire help with the farm work and offered employment to a local man. The "hired hand" seemed quite acceptable to the family but Pup didn't trust him. Unlike the family members whom the dog followed around the building area, wagging his tail in a friendly manner, he did not allow the stranger near him. But he did follow the hired man everywhere, remaining just out of reach.

Soon, it became equally obvious that the helper did not appreciate the dog's attention. He attempted to drive the animal away or order it to stay out of his way. Nothing deterred Pup's resolve as he relentlessly continued his watch of the man.

Then tools and equipment seemed to disappear. It had never been difficult to find tools before the arrival of the new help, but now nothing ever seemed to be where it belonged. Indeed, tools were often nowhere to be found.

At first, it was assumed that the items in question were merely mislaid. "No", said the hired hand, "I haven't seen them."

But he must have. The fence had been repaired and hammers and wire stretchers were missing. Repairs were completed on farm machinery and wrenches were gone. He must have seen them. He had either helped with the work or undertaken it on his own. He would have been forced to make use of the items in question.

Ben heard the questions at supper each evening, as his parents or older brothers spoke of missing items and blamed each other for their strange disappearance. But it made little difference. He and his dog knew exactly how they were being lost.

Soon, the shadowing was no longer necessary, as the hired man received his notice. He would no longer be around the farm. As more and more tools and supplies had disappeared, the probability of his thefts became too great. It could not be proven that he was responsible for the disappearing items but something had to be done. With his dismissal, the disappearance of equipment ended.

As hard as it seemed to believe, the man had glared at the dog when he departed. He blamed the animal for his demise but not a word was uttered. He accepted his situation. There was no other recourse.

One morning, it happened! Pup did not come to greet the boy at the door as he left the house to begin morning chores. Indeed, the dog was nowhere to be found. Ben was returning to the house for breakfast when he saw it.

The dog's tail was protruding beyond the corner of the house. He moved, carefully, toward the tail, intent on surprising the old dog.

The dog didn't move! He lay silent, his nose resting on the side of the unfinished dish of food. He was dead!

As the tears fell at the loss of his friend, the boy thought of the hired man.

Jay Bernard

A DAY AT THE COUNTY FAIR

Rush! Rush! Rush! The whole world seemed in a rush.

Mother and Father had awakened early to do the chores around farm. It was summer and today the whole family was going into town to the fair.

The County Fair is a very exciting place for young children with many things to see, touch and taste.

Oh, what pies they were! Why, the very aroma, drifting through the kitchen door and across the yard on a gentle summer breeze always caused the children, to drool, as they dreamed of the flavor of those pies, so sweet on the tongue. But, alas, only the judges would taste them. They could only sniff and dream, or eat the castaways whose appearance determined that they were not good enough to win a contest.

Finally, the chores were done, everything was packed and they were off to the fair. As young as they were, they couldn't keep still, they bubbled noisily as they passed over the rutted country roads toward town. The nearer they came to the fair grounds, the greater the anticipation grew.

Topping a small rise the fairgrounds came into view, a large sprawling ant hill with activity everywhere. The family's weathered car edged forward behind the line of vehicles, slowly approached the gate and passed through.

Once parked, mother hurried to enter her pie in the baking contest, three giggling girls running along beside her. Father, with the boys in tow, hurried toward the livestock barns to feed and water livestock entries, brought to the fair earlier, and to give each animal a final brushing.

With the livestock cared for, it was off again; back to meet the family group. Reunited, they would be free to enjoy the rides, after a final word of caution of course, and a reminder to meet their mother by the entry to the grandstand at three o'clock to watch the horse races.

There were so many rides and side shows on the midway, it was difficult to decide which to enjoy first. There was a Ferris wheel, roller coaster, rollo planes and dodge-'em cars for the bigger children and a merry-go-round for younger ones. And the side shows… Wow! There were men who could lift horses, fat ladies, tall men, bearded ladies and a lady motorcyclist who rode around in a large drum and right up the wall!

All too soon, three o'clock rolled around. The children left the midway to meet their mother. There were so many interesting things left to see and do; it seemed a shame to leave so early.

Upon arrival at the gate to the grandstand mother could be seen pushing hurriedly through the throngs of people, advancing toward the gate.

Seeing everyone she shouted gleefully, "I won! I won!"

She had won first prize in the baking contest with her apple pie. How proud she was, as she displayed her ribbon and allowed it to flutter in the breeze when she came to meet her family.

She grabbed the two younger children by the hands and rushed on, swept along with the crowd, inward to the very bowels of the cavernous grandstand enclosure.

"Don't get lost!" they heard their mother call and then, before anyone knew what was happening, they were safe in their seats, watching the riders exercising their horses and stretching their legs in preparation for the big race.

When the horses began to line up, the children's father rode to the centre of the track to take his position. The rail position would have been desirable, but centre track wasn't bad, as the race started on a straight away. If a horse was quick off the mark, his rider could move to the inside position before reaching the first corner.

The starter raised his arm, starting pistol in hand. Riders leaned forward in their saddles, horses straining forward against the pull of the bits in their mouths.

Bang! They were off, heading down the straight away, past the grandstand, hooves thundering as they went.

Father and Buck jumped first when the gun sounded and lead the pack, but were soon running shoulder to shoulder with Uncle Billy's mare as they passed the grandstand, already pulling ahead of the other horses.

The family sat frozen as the two horses matched strides, muscles rippling on powerful shoulders as each rider urged his mount on to greater effort.

They were quickly approaching the critical first turn, where the horse on the rail was expected to take the lead, and the two horses still ran neck and neck. They entered the turn. The family's hearts missed a beat, every second expecting to see Uncle Billy's mare move into the lead but she didn't. My gosh – she didn't! Father had urged Buck to give an extra effort and he had summoned the strength to come through the turn even. But, could he last? Could he maintain this torrid pace?

As the two horses thundered down the back straight, far out distancing the others, Buck continued to creep forward. Slowly but steadily, he took the lead and began to increase it. He was winning! Then, suddenly, as he passed through the final turn and headed down the home stretch, he seemed to tire, to falter. Oh No! The flying mare was passing, moving into the lead once again.

Hopes dropped as they watched their father lean forward and pat Buck's neck as they came through the turn. Why, it seemed Father was speaking to the proud old horse.

Suddenly, Buck was coming faster. Moving up again, thundering past the competition and crossing the finish line in a burst of speed such as they had never before witnessed. He had won!

Once the bedlam subsided, throngs of well wishers gathered by the stage, beside which stood the winning rider and Old Buck. It had been a close race and the family's horse had come out the winner. But what had spurred Buck on to the final charge?

Finally, the children just had to ask; "Dad, what did you say to Buck to make him run so fast? Were you talking to him?"

"No," said a beaming father. "He had given his best and I merely patted him. I guess he thought he could do better because he seemed to get a second wind and showed he was a better horse than I had given him credit for."

DRIVER TRAINING
ISN'T
FOR EVERYONE

In the mid nineteen twenties, it was normal for farm wives to care for the house and children and ensure there was a meal on the table at dinner time. The need to drive an automobile was not listed in their job descriptions and few did.

Not only was it not unique to the time for women to lack the skills needed for driving, it was rarely required. In fact, many seemed to lack the confidence, if not the composure necessary to master the automobile. But a few had goals - and foremost among them was learning to drive.

Sarah fell into the "would-be-driver" group. After traveling many miles on a horse drawn buggy, she felt it was time to upgrade her mode of transportation. She attempted to find driving instructors on many occasions but, through no fault of her own, found it difficult to arrange for instructors who had the patience required to withstand her nervous attempts to maneuver a motorized vehicle. Therefore, neighbors continued to be visited using horse and buckboard as transportation.

Sarah had no difficulty getting a car in motion and she did manage to steer between the fence posts on most occasions. Her main difficulties lay in shifting gears and the ability to stop. With no automatic transmissions in her day, she modified the situation to her needs. Whatever gear the car was in when it began to roll would do quite well for the entire trip.

Stopping, however, was more difficult to modify without damaging the car. And fences, trees or farm machinery were not considered a proper substitute for brakes.

Finally having found a suitor with patience and a new car, Sarah was now assured of success. Brand new cars of any type were difficult to come by and this one, a convertible, added to the pride of its young owner.

One sunny day, he appeared with a brand new Plymouth convertible to take his lady driving. The young man was extremely proud of his car and his ability to help. And, in spite of certain reservations, he agreed to allow his lady love to sit behind the wheel for her first lesson.

Wishing to gain her approval and to share his good fortune came first in his motivation as they left for their afternoon drive. Off they went to enjoy the fresh air and thrill of the open road.

Roads were often mere trails between trees and across the prairies, and journeys could be interrupted by gates as drivers attempted short cuts across fields.

On this particular Sunday, as luck would have it, our handsome couple happily motored along until they chanced upon a gate. No problem! Nothing unusual here! It was time for the driving lesson to begin. Being the perfect gentleman, the young suitor clambered down from the vehicle to open the barbed wire gate and requested his fair damsel to drive the car through the opening. His words, however, were, "When I get down, would you please drive the car through the gate?"

As his feet touched the ground, Sarah slid over and sat at the wheel, pressed the clutch pedal to the floor, placed the car in gear and released the clutch. The car moved smoothly forward and through the gate. She was so proud of her accomplishment… Unfortunately, her gentleman had neglected to inform her that the gate was to be opened first. She had not waited but taken him at his word, had responded quickly, and had driven the car through the unopened gate, barbed wire and all!

It was to be her last driving lesson for some time.

DRIVING IS STILL
NOT FOR EVERYONE

Mother! What a pleasant title! A special person, a special place in one's memory! Is it any wonder that a special day is held in her honour yearly?

One mother was, indeed, special. Not only to the children of the family but to everyone who knew her. A heart of gold rested within her tiny chest but it was the heart of a giant. Not that the woman was by any means of great physical stature. Indeed the heart was involved mainly with the accompaniment of an understanding mind, held neatly in a head that rose to a height of less than five feet from the floor.

In spite of this lack of stature, however, like most mothers she never hesitated to make one aware of her presence. She could be counted on to make her needs and desires well known to her husband and children. She was a simple woman from a simple upbringing, participating in a simple existence.

Her first attempt at driving a motor vehicle did not quite hit top marks with her instructor; nor was her next attempt any more successful. Driving home from the fields where her husband was harvesting she was forced to make the journey with no help except for that of her youngest son. Not being very sure of her ability to handle the situation, she placed the old car in first gear and began to head for home. No matter how anyone coaxed, begged or cajoled, she would not shift to the next gear which would allow the old car to travel faster which resulted in the entire trip being taken in first gear. Once she managed to get the car into gear and rolling, no amount of begging would convince her to tamper with a winning situation.

Slowly down the old road she went until the lane was reached, her husband and the tractor close behind. All went well until she turned right and slowly approached the parking area beside the house.

Upon preparing to stop, however, she pressed the brake hard with her right foot. Nothing happened, and the car continued through the parking area and began to nose down hill as it passed over a crest. When the brake failed to stop progress, Sarah moved her foot to the clutch but, since the car now headed down hill, it merely increased speed.

Noticing she was headed toward some farm machinery panic set in and she never regained enough composure to press two pedals at once. However, Sarah's son, not more than eight years of age managed to crawl onto the floor and bring the car to a halt before it struck any implements or sustained any permanent damage.

In general, she simply did not seem to understand machinery. Nor did she possess a quick sense of humour where the automobile was concerned.

Shortly after the automatic transmission became popular, it seemed common knowledge that one must push these vehicles some thirty miles per hour if it was necessary to get them to start. To Sarah, who was somewhat mystified by anything which dealt with automobiles, this was phenomenon; and being told the joke of the day, failed to amuse her in any way, particularly when it came from one of her sons.

"Mom", he said, "You know this fellow was stalled on the side of the road when a lady drove up the road and stopped to ask if he had any problems. He replied that his car required a push in order to start it but, since it had an automatic transmission, he must be going thirty miles per hour to be successful. Well, the man sat and waited and waited but nothing happened. So he looked in his rear view mirror and there came the lady, at thirty miles per hour!"

Sarah, the ever practical, looked at him in surprise, forgetting that the lady had been a motorist and said, "Don't be so silly. She couldn't run that fast!"

Jay Bernard

IT'S JUST HORSE PLAY

There he sat, perched lazily on the top rail of the corral. A small man in stature, he wore his hat at a jaunty angle to emphasize his presence. Fred may have been on the short side, but he portrayed the cocky attitude of a bantam rooster confidently in control of his flock.

But it wasn't a chicken coop he was watching. Inside the corral, a dozen horses, hooves pounding, created a whirlwind of dust that rose and settled on their surroundings. Close behind, a second herd followed. Several frustrated cowboys ran along shouting and waving their arms, the dust forming mud on their sweaty faces as they tried to force the horses through a barn doorway.

Fred had been minding his own business and enjoying the afternoon sun as he lay back under a tree until he had been drawn to the din. His curiosity had gotten the best of him and he had decided to check on the commotion. And check on it he did, first peering through the fence at passing horses and then climbing to his lofty perch for a better view.

Fred chuckled aloud. He remembered children running for the wooden horses on the merry-go-round at a recent fair as he watched the frustration build in the cowhands. It was obvious looking at their faces. They were tired and at wits end when it came to accomplishing the awesome task of guiding a stallion and his mares through a barn door.

He looked down from his perch and innocently asked, "You fellas havin' a little trouble?"

His innocent question struck a sour note with the lead hand, which saw it as sarcasm.

"What else?" he replied. "Kinda obvious isn't it?"

Fred tilted his hat a little more to one side.

"Tryin' to put 'em in the barn?" he asked.

The second question proved even more annoying to the lead hand. Indeed, he considered the useless banter nothing less than needling and found nothing funny in the situation. And to top it all off, there went that darn hat again, adjusted to even more of an angle as it threatened to lie on one ear.

"If you want 'em in the barn, just get out of the corral and we'll see what we can do," offered Fred.

This was a challenge the cowboys could not ignore. For nearly an hour they had given their best effort to gain control of the situation. It had seemed a simple task at the onset but frustration had set in as both horse and cowboy had lost their composure. With a signal to his men, the lead hand moved away and climbed over the rails, followed closely by the other cowboys.

In spite of following instructions and clearing the corral, the cowboys saw no reaction from the youthful stranger on the top rail. Instead of hopping down with the horses, he merely sat and watched.

Minutes passed and the wayward horses settled down and began to nuzzle each other, reassurance that all was as it should be. There was no further danger or harassment. The horses came to a standstill and Fred watched as their breathing returned to normal.

Finally, he reacted. He stretched leisurely, adjusted his hat and hopped into the corral. Slowly, he approached the stallion, speaking softly and keeping the sun at his back. His hand reached out and touched the horse's neck, caressing it in gentle strokes.

With the obvious rapport building, Fred began to stroke the horse's face and nose, allowing his scent to become familiar to the animal.

"C'mon fellas," he said, as he turned and walked through the barn door.

Without hesitation, the horses followed.

As he walked away from the corral, Fred heard the lead hand speak once more.

"Boys," he said. "I don't mind bein' bettered, but darn I hate that hat."

TURPENTINE PUP

It happened every day without fail. Like clock work, they would watch the dog on its way across the field to their farm. It came sniffing its way across the mile of pasture between their house and its home. And here it was again, coming slowly along the fence.

They had asked their neighbour a dozen times to please keep the dog home.

Regardless of what was tried, short of tying the animal up permanently, it would find its way to their house each afternoon, chase some of the chickens, irritate the resident dogs and make itself a nuisance.

The resident dogs proved to be good hosts and merely accepted him as a friend. But, he was no friend of the birds, the chickens or the livestock. And to the entire family, he was nothing but a pest. Several times he had chased the cattle, scattering them throughout the pasture and forcing their herders to round them up.

The previous day, the dog had been braver than usual. Chickens were chased around the yard until one was finally caught. They had become so used to his daily visits that the chickens felt he belonged there and felt no danger. However, when he caught the hen, he killed it; he would definitely need to be discouraged from further visits. Everyone could do without his mischief.

So when the farmer's sons looked across the pasture and saw him coming down again, they decided to put an end to these unwanted visits once and for all.

As the boys watched the dog approach, one of the brothers picked up a rope hanging on a fence post by the gate and walked over to the cattle's watering trough, to await the visitor's arrival. Needed supplies, an old wire brush and a dark coloured bottle of liquid had been readied to welcome the dog in the most unexpected fashion.

Finishing his journey, the mutt acted as though he had just arrived home rather than being an unwelcome visitor. Approaching the boys, tail wagging, he reassured them of his friendly intentions. One boy bent over and patted his head.

The oldest boy picked up the wire brush, while his brother picked up the dark bottle labelled in large letters, "TURPENTINE!" One quick swipe with the brush in the appropriate area, a splash of turpentine and the job was done. They carried out the procedure rapidly and without incident, then stood back to watch the result of their efforts.

Letting out one quick yelp when the turpentine found its mark, the dog took off as fast as he could run. And he was anything but choosy about the course he would follow. Rather than choosing the familiar pasture route, he headed straight into the wheat field at full speed. Confused by the height of the grain, the dog's straight line soon turned into circles. Although completely out of sight, the moving grain, showing his location. Finally, finding his bearing for home, the boys watched a straight line appear in the field. And straight it remained until he emerged into the security of his own yard, and home.

FROGS

As door catches clicked an ominous, cautious feeling crept into their souls. They had no way of knowing what destiny held for them. They only knew that the time for change had come and that they must chart a new course in their lives. And that could be described as a future far removed from their normal existence within the friendly confines of the city with which they were familiar.

Leaves were beginning to show on the trees, spring was finally adding contrast to the color as the earth awakened once more. The mountains rose, snow crowned, from behind the foothills in the distance, peaks glistening in the morning sun. Destiny beckoned to the travelers. A new future, a new life lay beyond these mountains.

Winding through the mountains, fatigue began to show on the face of the driver.

"Let's not travel too far today," he said. "There's no sense in being too tired tomorrow or our business may prove worthless."

A friendly motel beckoned from the right side of the highway.

"Great," the passengers agreed, "Let's stop here for the night."

Although rooms were arranged in short order, it seemed as though their heads had barely touched the pillows before a pounding came at the door. It couldn't possibly be morning already. But, it was! The voice assured the room's inhabitants of this fact.

"C'mon! Let's get goin'," it called. "It's time to hit the road!"

The day seemed short as pounding rain converted the sky to a dismal day. It was a furious bursting storm cloud descending from on high driven by strong winds.

As it worsened, stones seemed to bounce on the pavement. They thudded on the roof of the car and bounced with abandon off the windshield. Indeed, the down pour had become so heavy the windshield wipers could barely keep up. It must be rocks loosened from the hillside that were causing all the clatter, they weren't white and they weren't hail.

But the thumps were far too soft for rocks of that size. These rocks had legs, four of them. And they were not bouncing off the highway, they seemed to be jumping.

And jumping they were as the highway came alive in the car's headlights. The whole surface of the road seemed to be moving as frogs jumped in all directions.

It was raining frogs!

Few were ready to believe the story of the raining frogs when the young couple returned home, but they continued to tell their tale. At least it brought laughter. Years later, they were to discover it was the result of a well known phenomenon. It had, indeed, rained frogs, scooped from nearby ponds by the winds and dropped on the highway.

GERBER'S CREEK

A rooster crowed in the hen house. It was time for morning chores on the small farm. Ben pulled himself slowly out of bed and stretched, dressed and headed off to fetch the cows for milking. As he had popped through the kitchen door, into the bright sunlight, he gave a whistle and Buck, the family's big Collie, crawled, tail wagging, from under the front step.

Looking across the fields, he saw the crocuses tuning the hillside blue. He'd pick a bouquet of flowers for his mother later. But now it was time to get on with the chores and preparing himself for what promised to be a busy day.

The pasture stretched for a mile east of the house and Ben and the dog trotted across the field. Nearly an hour passed before the cows were herded into their stalls in the barn. With the milking completed, Ben was feeling hungry when his mother called for breakfast.

It was a special day. On Saturdays, Stan came for a visit; living only two miles down the road, he would soon arrive. The boys had a very special plan in mind. Riding their horses over to the big wood and exploring it and, perhaps, fishing in Gerber's Creek would be a fine way to while away the daylight hours.

Once Stan arrived, Ben picked up the lunch his mother had packed, saddled a pony and the boys headed for the big wood and Gerber's Creek.

They didn't really care if they explored the wood or not. They had done so many times and knew every path and twig. The main point of interest today however, lay with the trout in the cool clear waters of the creek which lazed along through the woods. And with the ice newly melted, it was time to land the big one.

They'd been warned many times against going to the creek but the boys knew just the path to take so old Mister Gerber wouldn't see them as they neared. Winding through the woods and opening into a little meadow where the creek formed a pond the temptation was too much to resist. There was little need to worry about Mr. Gerber; he couldn't see this pond unless he came through the woods.

Because he had caught them fishing in the stream before that day and the outcome was less than pleasing, the boys still worried a bit. Getting caught would be distasteful! How well they remembered the scolding they'd received the last time. Stan had just pulled a big trout out of the water when old Mr. Gerber jumped from behind a tree roaring, his face red with fury. "Now I've gotcha!" he cried. And got them, he had.

The boys had raced home and escaped the old man. But both sets of parents heard about it in detail and warned them of the possible consequences.

"You should know better than to go near Mr. Gerber's creek and bother the old man, even if it has the best fishing holes around", they were told. "Why must you always cause trouble with the neighbors?"

Yet, here they were, back again.

The fish in the stream didn't really belong to the old man but the land did. And the boys were not prepared to argue the point with a man known for his temper. He was old, but he stood over six feet tall, weighed two hundred pounds and was a frightening sight to behold when he bellowed from behind his scraggy beard.

But, this time he would not catch them. The boys felt confident as they reached the hidden pond, dismounted their horses and began to unpack the fishing tackle. Nevertheless, as they settled to their poaching task, they jumped at each crackling twig or the rustle of the wind in the new leaves.

"Could that be old Mr. Gerber?"

"No! Of course not…"

They shrugged the fears away and resumed fishing.

64

Fishing was good and soon the boys began to feel at ease, gaining more confidence as they pulled one giant after another from the water.

Suddenly, Stan whispered, "What's that?" A rustle came from the bushes in the direction of the Gerber house.

The noise grew louder until it was beside the pond, right beside the boys! The morning exploded with a fury!

"Ha, Ha" bellowed Mr. Gerber, "Again!"

Grabbing their fishing gear the interlopers ran for the horses, leaving most of their fish behind. The boys had time to make their getaway, but had no chance to retrieve the creel of fish cooling in the creek.

Horses charged along the twisting trail leading out of the big wood, the boys too frightened to look back.

As time, and distance between them and the creek grew, they began to think rationally once more. They remembered the fish cooling in the creek! The creel! Oh, would Dad be angry! They must get the creel! Surely Mr. Gerber couldn't have found it yet!

Stopping their horses, dismounting and tying them to trees, it was time to make a plan.

"We gotta get the rest of the stuff without bein' seen," said Ben.

Stan agreed. All went well until they neared the pond. As they came to the edge of the meadow, they stopped dead, a chill racing up their spines. The pair stared in disbelief at the scene in the meadow. There lay Mr. Gerber, basking in the sun, his hand so close to the stream that it almost touched the creel.

The boys would be forced to entice the old man to leave the creek. Asking for the fish would certainly be of little use. The problem was; he seemed so comfortable he may remain in his present position for the rest of the day.

Being caught by Mr. Gerber again was out of the question. This time they might not be so lucky and punishment (not a warning) would be in store.

Luck was grazing in the meadow. To their good fortune, Daisy, the Gerber's old cow, stood munching on the spring grass, her bell jingling each time she raised her head to survey her surroundings.

"The bell!" said Ben. "Let's get Daisy's bell!"

"Why?" asked Stan. "What good can an old brass bell possibly do us now?"

"You simpleton," Ben replied. "You take the bell and wander through the woods. Mr. Gerber will likely follow and I'll grab the fish. Meet you at the edge of the trees."

Going into action, Stan gently slipped the bell off Daisy. With the bell firmly in his hand, off he jingled through the woods, hoping Mr. Gerber was close behind. It worked. The old man followed the retreating bell.

Now was the time! Ben ran to the creek and pulled the creel from the water. Happily, he jogged along, on his way to the end of the trail. Stan was waiting, doubled over in laughter. At Ben's approach, Stan jingled the bell once again, and laughed even harder.

It was late in the afternoon when they reached home and the boys told Ben's parents their story while they cleaned the fish. It was best to tell the parents first as the neighbor would probably mention it anyway. Trouble was trouble; but why not limit the punishment as much as possible?

"I've warned you before about going near that creek," said Ben's father. "Maybe a lesson is in order. You insist on fishing even though you know it upsets Mr. Gerber? Maybe you boys should ride over to his house and invite him for dinner. That way we can at least share the fish."

Giving up fishing seemed a better option.

HORSES BUCK DON'T THEY?

There was no doubt about it. He was in the mood for a little horseback riding, and since he didn't own a horse; that meant a trip to his uncle's farm and a visit with his cousin Stanley.

It took a bit of begging and whining, but after a short while, Ben finally convinced his older brother to give him a ride the three miles between the two farms for the visit. Stan was, as always, happy to see him.

They had talked about the upcoming adventure at school throughout the week. Stan was sure his brother's horse was the fastest in the country but Ben disagreed. True, he had no horse of his own on which to bet but there was still Old Flo and in his memory he had never known her to be beaten.

Shortly after Ben's arrival, the race planning was complete. The boys caught the two horses easily and put them on bridles.

Saddles were optional equipment and the cousins always preferred to take the simple course. Just grab a handful of the horse's mane and vault on. Riding bareback was second nature to the boys. And when the horses felt the pull on their mane, they always assisted by turning under the rider.

But before this day was through, there was cause to have second thoughts on the saddle issue.

The chosen race track was a straight away through a hay field, a narrow cut of grass between fields of grain which were standing high and just beginning to turn to gold as the summer wore on. It was ready made for the occasion and both boys agreed it would do nicely. The stretch was only half a mile in length but would allow the horses to get up speed and show their abilities without any danger of winding them. It was a fair test to determine the fastest horse.

As the pair prepared to start their race, Stan threw in one last rule.

"Just to give ourselves a test," he said. "Let's start standing on the ground, get on and then race."

With his cousin the far more experienced rider, Ben looked for alternatives but Stan was adamant. Finally, the agreement was made on the basis that it would be Ben who said "Go!" At very least, he thought this advantage would even out the situation.

"Where's the finish line?" Ben asked.

"Let's put it right at that clump of trees near the end of the field," Stan replied.

With the rules agreed upon, the boys lined their horses up behind an imaginary line and prepared for the mount and the race.

"Go!" Ben shouted and the two leaped into the air, landing astride horses already making their first jump and breaking into full flight.

Heads low, one hand grasping reins and the other a horse's mane, the racers thundered off across the field. The horses were in full flight in an instant; ears locked back and throwing clods of grass in their wake.

As Stan's horse edged forward, Ben felt he may have been wrong. His conclusion had been based on the fact that Flo had once been a trail horse that led the trek and didn't like anything ahead of her. She would give it her best effort, but this time her best may not be good enough. He urged her on with a soft kick to the ribs but it was of little use. She was already doing her best.

Suddenly Ben was looking at a horse's tail as Stan's steed began to pull away. He'd lose. There was no doubt about that.

But life does have its way of throwing curves and disrupting the obvious. Not every outcome will be as predicted – certainty becomes uncertainty.

Stan's horse cut sharply to the right, barely clearing the way for Ben and the charging Flo. It was going at right angle to the agreed course and headed straight for the grain field.

In utter amazement, Ben reined in his horse and watched.

As it reached the edge of the grain, Stan's charger seemed to lose any desire to run. It dug its front feet into the dirt sharply and gave a small buck, barely raising its back feet from the ground. The horse stood still but the rider became an instant projectile.

Headfirst off his steed, Stan flew, headed for the grain. In an instant, he disappeared with the only sign of him being the rippling of the grain.

Ben was worried; he trotted his horse over to the edge of the golden sea and waited. Stan could be hurt.

He wasn't. This day's fate would be on the side of his cousin. Unhurt but slightly bewildered, Stan stood up in the chest high grain, a strange look on his face, a bridle in one hand and a handful of his horse's mane in the other. He was fine, just a bit shaken by the whole experience.

But for Ben, the race wasn't over. With his cousin unhurt, he turned his horse and calmly crossed the finish line before returning to Stan, no longer able to control his laughter.

"I won!" he said.

Stan, of course, disagreed. But rules are rules and this was one they hadn't covered. The win would stand. Especially when one considered that Stan wasn't up to an instant replay.

THE HOLIDAY

A holiday is exactly what one makes of it. It does not have to be an excursion to Mexico, Hawaii or even Disneyland. It can be as simple as spending time in one's own backyard.

When Ben was a youngster in junior high school, Disneyland had just begun and was a relatively new and exciting place for families to spend their holidays. Many of his classmates planned for months and talked among themselves prior to a Disneyland adventure. Most children, however, listened and dreamed but knew that ever seeing such a glamorous sight with their families was impossible.

At hearing classmates speak of their exciting times, when they returned from lengthy holidays to far away places, Ben was often envious. He would talk of this as the family sat around the supper table. His brothers and his sister, somewhat older than him, expressed their thoughts freely.

"Don't worry about it. We never went on a holiday and we haven't lost anything by staying here," they said.

This, however, did not stop him from dreaming and expressing his feelings on the subject from time to time.

Finally, Ben's father decided that they would take a family holiday. Not a long one but a holiday nevertheless, to the mountains. For a period of two weeks prior to the trip, Ben was very excited although he never spoke of his holiday to anyone, since his friends would not see a one day outing as anything worth mentioning. To Ben, it was the chance of a lifetime, something that had never been a part of family life in his house.

The family awoke very early on Sunday morning, packed the car with enough food for lunch and soon they were on their way. As they drove along the highway, they played a variety of games. Name the make of car coming towards them was always a favourite. Who could tell its name the farthest away? Then they went on to a game of 'I Spy'. All the time they played, the car whizzed down the highway at fifty five miles per hour.

"Always drive five miles under the speed limit," their father cautioned on many occasions, "It's safer and you'll never get a speeding ticket."

He was, probably, correct but when one is excited, it would seem more enjoyable to travel five miles per hour over the speed limit rather than under it.

Nonetheless, the family arrived at their destination by nine in the morning and the view was spectacular. The sun still hung in the east, not yet reaching the pinnacle of its day's journey and the snow capped mountains were towers glimmering in the sun. How tiny one felt in comparison!

After touring the town site, swimming in the hot springs, walking beside a buffalo paddock and visiting with several friendly squirrels it was time to move on. They settled down in a park to eat their lunch in the fresh air. Even this was an experience since the only time they had ever eaten outdoors was during threshing in the fall.

Everything tasted so good, but they were in a hurry. Their father had promised to drive up one of the mountain roads to visit a lake, part way up the ridge. They packed the remains of their lunch, placed it in the trunk and climbed into the nineteen fifty Plymouth, ready for the journey.

Up the mountain road they went, looking back as the town disappeared and the valley growing wider and wider beneath them. They wound higher until their mother saw a pull-off, with some deer grazing nearby.

"Stop," she said. "I want to take a picture."

She hauled out the camera and clicked away. The photo session was cut short, however, when Ben's sister Mary pointed to a little fawn and asked if mother would like a closer picture of it.

"Of course," mother replied.

Mary took some bread from a brown bag and held it out the open car door. Much to everyone's surprise, the fawn approached the car. Then Mary shortened her reach to lure the animal closer but, shocking everyone, further temptation was not necessary as the little deer calmly crawled right into the back seat of the car. Now mother had her close look at a fawn.

With the fawn finally pushed out of the car, the family continued up the road until they came upon the most beautiful, crystal clear, emerald coloured lake Ben had ever seen. He crept close to the edge of a rock and looked down. The lake was fifty feet deep even by the shore and he could see through the crystal waters right to the sandy bottom. There on the bottom lay several massive fish, basking in the sun and worrying about absolutely nothing. Their world was at peace.

All too soon it was time to board their vehicle to continue the journey. Back down the mountain and into the valley they went. It seemed unfortunate, but their father said it was time to start homeward.

As they exited the park gates, two large black bear were blocking the highway, begging from passengers in the cars that went by, ever so slowly.

"Don't put your hand out and feed them," mother warned. "They look nice and seem friendly but they're still wild animals."

Around a curve in the road, traffic had come to a halt again. Was it more bears? No, this time it was a flock of mountain sheep, wandering about in the ditches, even standing on hill sides that seemed to rise almost straight up from the edge of the road. Posing for pictures and begging food from everyone who passed seemed to keep them quite happy.

"May we get out and have a closer look?" the children asked.

The sheep were amazingly friendly. They nuzzled hands with their noses and, if one continued to ignore them, bumped gently until they had your attention and you were prepared to feed them something. It seemed they would eat anything!

But with handouts running out, aggression built. The gentle bumps became butts until a ram backed away a few feet and charged. A car door buckled under the impact and added significantly to the cost of the simple holiday. Disneyland may have been a cheaper choice.

But the family had proven something. They had proven that a successful holiday depends upon the expectations of those involved. If one expects huge vacation trips, that is what is necessary to have an enjoyable time. But, if one expects nothing, a simple one day holiday can be as exciting as any other. At least, they had been on a holiday.

HARDY

Many years ago, before combines were in common use on the prairies, farmers could not move about their fields picking up their crops. Instead, threshing of grain was carried out with stationary equipment, to which the bundles of grain were hauled on horse drawn wagons.

Children on the farms loved to see the threshing crews arrive as it meant times of story telling, dancing and singing in the evening hours. The men who gathered with the threshing crews came from all over the world; so many an interesting tale were told. Whether or not the stories were true only the narrator knew for certain.

One threshing season, little knowing this fall would hold great differences; one family waited anxiously for the threshing crew to arrive at their farm. The grain stood in stooks, creating golden tepees in the fields. The father was impatient to have it in the bins before the frosts came or the dreaded snows fell. At last, on a beautiful day in September, the threshing machine came up the long lane, pulled by a tired, gasping old tractor. The men had arrived for the harvest!

The children stood in the yard watching the machines, wagons, men and horses as they neared the farm buildings. Wow! This meant the cooks who made such fantastic pies would slip a favourite, apple, blueberry or lemon, out behind the cook house and quietly give them to the children. And, all you had to do was sneak one of Mom's pie plates out of the kitchen.

As they watched the men pass, the youngsters became more and more excited. Then, suddenly, they saw a sight they had never before set eyes on! Could they believe our eyes? Why, one of those men was as black as the coal that heated the house in winter.

Hardy, (for that they were to learn) was his name, was a giant of a man. Standing over six feet tall with very broad shoulders, he towered above the rest of the crew. And he carried himself with obvious pride. But most impressive of all was his broad smile, which exposed teeth that glistened like pearls.

By noon, the threshing crew was hard at work and sheaves of grain were being hurled into the cavernous mouth of the threshing machine to be engorged by the metal beast and spit out into an ever growing pile of straw. The children watched the men work as beads of perspiration gathered on their brows, then streamed down their faces in rivulets. At sunset, the work stopped and the wagons raced toward the barn.

What a cloud of dust they raised as the teams of horses thundered up the small hill and passed the house. Each man wished to be first to feed his team, being sure to reach the table in time for the mouth watering meal mother and the cooks would serve.

The children ran to the barn to watch the horses being fed and watered. Only something seemed wrong. Hardy, with his friendly smile, wasn't hurrying.

"Aren't you hungry?" He was asked.

"Yes," Hardy replied, "But a man only earns his feed if he's worked a full day."

At supper time, Hardy, true to his word, did not enter the cook house. Instead, he sat on the porch playing with the dog until everyone had finished eating.

The children, finishing supper quickly, rushed out to speak with the big man. In the next few minutes, many questions were asked. "Why aren't the palms of your hands black? Why are you so big? Why do you have white spots on your arm? Why is your hair white?"

Hardy, in his inimitable manner, attempted to answer the questions as they asked them. He told everyone about his color and his hands, but the children were certain he had worked so hard the black had rubbed off. Most intriguing were the white marks on his arm. Time after time, he was asked about them but Hardy wasn't ready to offer any explanation.

In time Hardy told many stories about his life; he became more comfortable and told of his growing up under extreme prejudice and suffering knife wounds. He came from Virginia where his grandfather had been a slave on a plantation, many years before. Why, even his father, who was much older than Hardy, had been born into slavery but he could remember little as he had been extremely young when slavery ceased.

From dawn to dusk Hardy and the men kept busy in the fields. Breakfast was served early every morning and during the day, mother ventured to the fields three times. The trek was made at mid-morning and mid-afternoon, with huge pots of coffee and buns, and at noon hour when she brought the men their lunch. The noon break was longer, half an hour, and during this time everyone gathered near the threshing machine to eat, let the noisy machines cool and the horses rest.

It was during these breaks that Hardy told many of his tales as everyone gathered around him to listen. One day, at last, he told how the white spots had appeared on his arm. Once while harvesting, Hardy had fallen from his hay rack while feeding grain into the hopper of the thresher and his arm had been caught in the belts and gears that ran the machine. He had been lucky, he said. His weight had been enough to cause the belts to slip on the pulley and kill the tractor engine. It had saved his arm from being crushed and perhaps saved his life. Only a few white marks remained as reminders of that day.

A great many things were learned from Hardy; how to make sling shots, how to drive horses and how to make wooden whistles from willows were among the best.

One afternoon, after delivering lunch to the men, one of child's dreams was fulfilled. He was permitted to remain in the field and ride with Hardy, keeping him company as he hauled loads of sheaves to the threshing machine. A whole afternoon with Hardy! What fun it was!

The work of the threshing crew drew, all too quickly, to a close and they soon moved on to the next farm. The children begged their father constantly, during those last fleeting days, to make Hardy stay, to no avail.

'When the threshing crew leaves, so must Hardy', they were told. And so it was.

For many months to come, the children relived Hardy's tales, world travels and stories of the Mexican Revolutionary War among them. They waited in vain for Hardy's return next season, as their father had promised.

But for Hardy and the children, the next season never came.

LADDIE

Darkness had fallen on the farm and everyone, except his father, was in the house. Having traveled to a town several miles away to attend an auction sale he had not yet returned. It was getting late, past the supper hour. Where could he be?

Headlights had appeared over the hill where the lane wound toward the house. Perhaps this would be him. The vehicle stopped outside and you could hear the engine sputter and die. Quiet resumed and everything was still.

Soon he heard footsteps on the wooden floor of the porch and the outer door closing. The inside door opened and his father entered the lighted room, carrying a small, cardboard box. Something seemed to be moving inside the closed lid. The box seemed to give a quiet, but audible, yip!

His father walked across the room and gently handed him the box.

"It's for you," his father said. "I hope it will help you forget the old dog."

"Open it!" the older man ordered.

Setting the box on a chair and unfolding the upper flaps, he felt the anxiety grow along with his curiosity as he waited to see what was inside. Suddenly, the top popped open and there, his front feet on the side of the box, his mouth open in a grin, was a brown puppy.

"What are you going to name him?" asked his father. "He's all yours you know!"

The child was ecstatic. He lifted the little fellow out of the box, holding it in his arms while the puppy licked at his face.

"I think we'll call him Laddie," the boy told everyone.

"Laddie it is!" said his father. "But, since we don't allow dogs in the house, you had better put something for him in the porch where he'll be warm and safe until morning."

It was difficult for the boy to sleep, as he lay in bed planning the experiences that awaited him and his little dog. The youth was twelve years old and very much in need of a friend, since there were no children of his age living in the neighbourhood. This dog would do just fine.

"We will", he convinced himself, "grow to be fine friends."

As the months passed, Laddie grew larger and peppier. One morning, after he and his young master had fetched the milk cows together several mornings in a row bringing them in to the barn for milking, the boy went out to call the pup intending to head back to the pasture as usual when he heard him barking. Looking up, he saw the cows coming through the gate and into the corral, followed closely by Laddie. He had finished the job without waiting for either company or instruction.

Two years passed quickly. The young boy was then old enough to legally, use a twenty two calibre rifle and was allowed to go on hunting excursions alone. Well, not exactly, alone, since he rarely went anywhere without his pal, who had grown into a loyal and loving companion. They trudged through brush or across open fields for hours on end, often leaving early in the morning and returning only at supper time.

As time passed, Laddie learned to crawl on his belly with his nose between his friend's heels, to pull his body quietly along when approaching wild game. He seemed to think like a human, always knowing exactly what was expected of him. Once his master stopped moving, the pup would maintain a perfectly motionless pose, waiting patiently for the report of the twenty two which, usually, meant there was a bird to be retrieved.

No one taught the dog to retrieve birds. He had merely watched unsuccessful attempts to retrieve a duck which had fallen into a slough and had instinctively deduced how he could help. He understood the problem!

A problem with the area where the family lived was the proximity to the local cemetery. Indeed, one climbed about two hundred yards up a hill from their house, to the spot where the lane met the road and, right across the road was the graveyard. It sent chills running the length of the boy's spine any time he had to walk home alone after dark. It was so frightening that children often chose the longer and completely darkened back approach to their home, across open fields and along groves of trees.

Once, while returning home after dark, he was certain white ghosts were frolicking on the cemetery grounds, running in and out among the grave stones, silhouetted in the bright moonlight. He ran! He ran for home as fast as his legs could carry him. However, moments of embarrassment had followed the next morning when he was instructed to find some missing geese. The identity of the ghosts became obvious.

In spite of parental reassurances that "There is no such thing as a ghosts;" it was difficult to put the experience with the geese to rest. He was convinced that each time he passed the darkened graveyard, something, or someone would be hiding behind the hedges, watching his approach and waiting patiently until their victim was close enough to pounce. What did parents know? He was certain that spirits lurked beyond that hedge, waiting to speed up someone's plans to join their number.

Only his trusted Laddie had had the magical powers to keep him safe. He called the dog as he neared the cemetery and was met by a wagging tail which always brought reassurance. With Laddie along nothing could frighten or hurt him, he thought. He made the world safe!

These nightly trips showed the dog where the farm's pigs and geese could wander and he soon began bringing them home, without direction, anytime they escaped from their pens. The family could be occupied with their daily activities when suddenly they would be disrupted by the insistent barking of Laddie signalling them to open the gates and allow entry to another escapee.

The most difficult animal on a farm to chase, especially if it has other plans in mind, is a pig. Pigs seem to sense when one is attempting to pen them and insist on keeping their freedom. Sows, with piglets, become mean and will attack any human that bothers them or their young. Surely, no one would be so irrational as to challenge a full grown sow.

This situation had been experienced many times by the boy but with Laddie, there was an answer. Laddie frustrated the pigs so badly they would willingly return to any pen in an effort to escape mental anguish. The dog would nip at a pig's hind feet and, when his victim spun around to defend herself, he would jump nimbly over the back and nip the opposite foot. Eventually the pig would be willing to find the gate to its pen rather than suffer further frustration.

Unfortunately, the nightly trips also brought about Laddie's demise. With something brown killing his hens, a neighbour was certain the boy's dog was the guilty party and lodged a complaint. It was a tough decision as the boy was certain coyotes were the problem but, in spite of his efforts, the decision was made to tie up the dog during the day or night unless the boy was there to accompany him in his escapades.

Having been free to roam at will, the loss of freedom affected Laddie. He soon became mean and protective and would challenge any stranger coming near. Only the length of chain saved many visitors from being bitten.

At last, there was no choice. The local "Dog Man" who dealt with animals, usually obtaining them free and selling them to the next owners, was brought on the scene. When told of Laddie's abilities, the man was quick to take up the offer of a free dog.

Soon Laddie was loaded into an old car and it began to roll off into the distance. As it topped the hill at the end of the lane, the boy took one last look and, in spite of his 14 years, he cried.

Jay Bernard

HAPPINESS
(COMES IN A BROWN PACKAGE!)

After the loss of one pal after another, happiness was not swift in coming for Benny. Indeed, losing one pal to sabotaged food and a second to a stranger did not sit well with the boy.

Nor did living in an old house with aged parents and few human friends. Dogs as friends had been the answer and now he had lost the only friends he really trusted. True, there had been an obnoxious mutt along the way which had been meant to fill the gap, but the experiment had proven a total failure. It was impossible to replace the emptiness left by the loss of a close buddy with an ill tempered stranger.

It was true. Perhaps he had not given the bulldog a chance. But why should he. The ugly cur didn't want to live with him so why would he try to win over the affection of the scruffiest animal he had ever laid eyes on? How could they even call that thing a dog? He certainly didn't measure up to any dog Benny had known. And he was anything but friendly.

Then, one crisp winter day Benny's lot in life seemed to take a decided turn for the better. His father arrived home just before dark, opened the door of the old Studebaker sedan and out jumped Brownie. His appearance was very much like that of one of his past buddies, which added to the pleasure of the moment. At first he thought Laddie had been returned to him, but, when he took a closer look he knew this was a far different dog. It mattered not, as the little fellow proved to be very friendly and ran up to him at once. "Yes, he'd do," thought the boy.

"His name is Brownie," said Benny's father. "I found him at the auction mart today and some fellow was giving him away."

But Ben wasn't listening to his father. He had already encircled the bundle of fur with his arms and was hugging it like a little boy may hug a favourite toy. The pup thrived on the attention and couldn't seem to get enough of it. It was love at first sight, the way life should be, a boy and his dog.

As the weeks passed, the new found friend proved to be a quick learner. He was, probably, not as intelligent as he was given credit for. But, he had other traits that were preferable to those the boy remembered of his past dog. The two thrived on being together and once again happiness had returned to the house. Once again, the boy went on day long hikes with his trusty twenty-two and his dog.

Brownie never learned to retrieve animals when they were shot, but he was a loving companion who never left his young master's side. They spent as much time playing tag, as they passed through the woods behind the farm buildings, as they did looking for something to shoot.

For two full cycles of the seasons, the boy and his dog enjoyed their freedom together. But, just after the lad reached his sixteenth birthday, it happened. One evening his father came home and announced that the farm had been sold. The family was moving into town.

Plans were made to move with the only suitable accommodation they could locate being a basement suite. Most of the furniture was sold and it seemed there would be no possible way they could keep the dog. The boy begged and begged until a solution was finally reached. Being kind hearted the new landlady had agreed that Brownie could be left tied to the bushes at the back of the lot.

With the move to town and the distance from the woods, the daily romps were reduced to a minimum. They lessened steadily in the early weeks of the change and finally became nearly none existent.

Fear crept in. The arrangement for Brownie wouldn't last much longer. Far too many stray dogs roamed the neighbourhood and a tied dog would be no match for them in a fight. It was feared they would attack Brownie during the night and injure him badly or even kill him. A few weeks passed with Ben, (he now preferred the shortened name since he was growing up), clinging to his friend. But his love for the dog finally won. He would allow Brownie to be given away to a good home.

With only one telephone call his life changed once again. "The Dog Man" arrived and was overjoyed with the situation.

With tears in his eyes, the boy shared one last parting hug with his friend before Brownie was placed into the old car and disappeared from his sight and life forever.

It was difficult to adjust to urban living and once again the boy experienced loneliness. His dog had been taken from him and this time, at the age of sixteen, he was left to fend for himself in a dreary suite while his parents took jobs in other towns. School suffered, he suffered and, most of all, he dreamt of Brownie and he cried.

Eventually, the tears stopped, but it was the last time any dog would share his life.

Jay Bernard

MOM'S ARE SPECIAL!

Many of life's favourite experiences revolve around mothers and their loving nature. And mothers of four or five decades ago were exactly that, with a touch of simplicity added. They asked for little except happiness and, in many cases that is all they got. However, they often rate high as unforgettable characters.

Children resorted to amusing themselves with tricks played upon unsuspecting mothers. Perhaps it was helpful in breaking the daily humdrum of farm life. Whatever it was, mothers often became the butt of many a young boy's humour.

Once felt that rubbing Listerine into the scalp would aid in the reduction of dandruff, one mother faithfully worked on her scalp while sitting beside the wooden kitchen table. She would sprinkle drops of the liquid on her scalp and massage it thoroughly into the tissues. It was during these sessions, the opportunity for humour often surfaced.

Indeed, it was not uncommon for her son to lean over quietly and replace the cap on the Listerine bottle, before setting the container exactly where it had been near at hand. His mother would pick it up several times, going through the motions thinking that she was putting more liquid on her head and rubbing it in – without once looking at the bottle. For the next ten minutes, she would continue to treat her scalp without noticing the cap was in place...

The lack of running water, electricity, or a sewage disposal system on the farm offered even more opportunity for merriment.

All liquid waste from the kitchen was poured into a five gallon pail in the corner of the kitchen and placed out of sight, behind the front door. When brushing teeth, it was necessary to move it slightly toward the centre of the room to allow freedom of movement.

One morning, Ben's mother was about to brush her teeth and moved the pail to a better location. While she was occupied, someone altered her plan by substituting the toothpaste tube with a tube of his father's shaving cream. Totally unaware of the switch, she calmly squeezed some of its contents; about an inch in length, on her tooth brush, placed it in her mouth and began to brush vigorously.

The result was amazing. Soon after beginning the process, she began to foam at the mouth, spit into the pail and finally ceased any attempt at brushing. She was far too occupied with her spitting to brush. Indeed, the more she spit, the more she foamed and the more she foamed, the more she spit. Several minutes later, the excitement subsided but, rest assured, no one was willing to admit to being the culprit who switched tubes.

The nature of Ben's mother was that of a worrier. She worried about everything! Was there enough to eat when guests arrived? Did they enjoy the food? Was there enough money to purchase the items the family required? Would the grocery store extend credit?

Of course, the most important question of all. "Did you put on clean underwear before leaving home, just in case of an accident and a trip to the hospital?"

The bottom line was, his mother had no sense of humour and took everything seriously. On one occasion, his brother decided to tell her a joke. And getting the punch line was never one of her strong points.

The advent of the automatic transmission in cars made the whole thing even more difficult for her to grasp.

"Mom," he said, "A lady came upon a man with a new car stalled beside a road and asked if she could help."

"Sure," said the stranded motorist. "But you'll have to be going thirty miles an hour for it to do any good."

"The driver waited and waited but nothing happened. Then he looked back and here came the lady, doing thirty miles an hour."

Not grasping the situation thoroughly, mother looked at him in astonishment and, forgetting the lady's car blurted, "Don't be silly. She couldn't run that fast."

No, mothers may not always be perfect. Indeed, in the eyes of their children they may even go so far as to be somewhat amusing as they seem outdated. They worry endlessly about things we are certain could never happen. But they wear the title of "Mother" extremely well and do it proud.

Here's to all those dedicated mothers wherever they may be.

MICE!

The snows had arrived early, catching the farm family unprepared. The grain had been cut and bound into sheaves, even stooked, but then luck failed. The early snow had arrived prior to the arrival of the threshing crew.

A second curse came. The mouse population exploded. Mice scurried everywhere, carving pathways, from stook to stook while staying warm beneath the snows. There was no chance of drying now! The grain had been frozen in place, a home and haven for the mice.

For many years, coyotes had been hunted for their pelts or shot as menaces to the farm animals. This year they were welcomed. Nothing could counter the mouse invasion without help from the coyotes. And the livestock would be perfectly safe.

Daily, the coyotes frolicked through the fields near the little farm house, hopping from stook to stook, burying their noses and reappearing with a mouth filled with the furry rodents. On some occasions, even more than one mouse would disappear at a single swallow as the coyote located a nest.

The farmer's youngest son, Bennie, was determined to help the coyotes, and the family, to save the crop. With great effort, he moved a large tractor tire toward the fields. Carefully laying it on its side to ensure the prison would hold its inmates, he began to search under bundles and snow to locate his quarry, the mice.

It seemed there were millions of the little, furry, grey creatures. As he moved a bundle, a mouse would run out, attempting to find shelter from this new enemy, but to no avail. Thanks to warm days, the snow was melting slightly and patches of the ground were soft, not yet frozen before the snows had fallen.

Carefully, the boy would run after a mouse, place his foot gently on its head, then reach down and pick it up by the protruding tail. The mouse was harmless. It could neither squirm upward enough to get a grasp on the youngster's hand to deliver a bite in its own defence nor squirm away. There was no means of escape.

He carried each mouse, systematically, to his tire prison and dropped it in. The first mouse seemed confused and attempted to gain freedom, soon discovering its escape was an impossible task. The rubber prison was simply impenetrable. Then, as other mice joined the first, they seemed to quiet down and accept their situation.

As the sun rose on the crisp countryside the following day, the youngster again returned to the fields to carry on his work as a hunter in search of big game. Perhaps they were really mice but, to him they had become big game on the plains of Africa.

Still some reality remained and he was convinced that he alone would save the crops. The day passed in an uneventful manner with the exception of one little beast which had disappeared at the very moment he felt sure of securing it. Where it went, he had no idea.

His activities continued until he was called for supper. As instructed by his mother, he washed his hands and face thoroughly to remove any germs the mice may carry and sat at the table, awaiting the meal.

Then the strangest thing happened! He felt his belt move! No! That was impossible! Belts can't move! But it did.

"Sit still and eat nicely!" urged his father.

He tried. But try as he would, his belt, right in the centre of his lower back continued to move about.

"Mom!" he said, "Something is moving in my back!"

"Outside! Quick!" she said.

The mother opened the belt and loosened his pants from his waist. Out fell the disappearing mouse which, as soon as it hit the ground, scrambled for safety.

"That does it!" the boy's mother said, feeling a bit weak. "There will be no more mouse chasing! Do you understand?"

The boy assured his mother that he understood and, after a thorough bath, "To rid yourself of the germs mice carry", as his mother had explained it, the boy went to bed.

For the next few days, as the warm weather continued to melt the snow, he watched the coyotes pursue mice, many of which could have been his former prisoners. He did not, however, venture back into the mouse infested fields until a few days prior to Christmas when the snow finally melted enough to carry out the harvesting operations.

It took a while before the great white hunter pursued the African beasts in the prairie wild lands.

INTRODUCTION
OF THE SHREW

The boy had spent several days catching mice since the early snows, each day seeing how many of the creatures he could capture. It was only a game as he let them free at the end of the day. His father had urged him to destroy the furry, grey creatures but he didn't have the heart to carry out such harsh instructions.

Nothing brought an end to his activities. He had taken a break over the period of a few days but had, once again, joined the coyotes in the field to see how many of the tiny creatures he could capture in a single day.

Today, he would set a record. He would capture more mice than ever before.

His imagination ran wild, as he pretended to be a famous bounty hunter, hot on the trail of imaginary criminals, the capture of which would result in large rewards. There were many rewards for well known criminals, whose faces graced the wall of every post office and sheriff's office from Tombstone to Deadwood. He knew – he'd seen them in his comic books.

The mice were the criminals. As he chased them through the swathes, catching them by the tails and depositing them in the tractor tire prison, he named them.

"Gotcha, Jesse James."

"There! That will teach you, you Daltons."

One famous gang after another was imprisoned.

As the day progressed, he counted his prisoners, twenty, forty, sixty, one hundred and more. It was, indeed, going to be a successful day.

He had captured in excess of one hundred famous outlaws before his mother forced him to break for lunch. It was a quick lunch and he was back to his duties. This day he would free the west. He would exceed two hundred prisoners.

As he resumed, a small but very quick foe emerged from under a swath and headed, for cover under the snow. A kick from the bounty hunter, and the snow cleared, revealing the escaped villain, quivering and searching for another avenue of escape. The boy bent over, grabbed the tail, and there dangled the villain.

It was a vicious looking outlaw, maybe Billy the Kid, differing noticeably in appearance from the rest and being somewhat smaller in stature. His face was sharp, pointed, with a much longer snout. The mouth opened and, rather than a squeak, a far different sound was heard as the trapped scoundrel displayed rows of sharp teeth.

Carefully, he turned the dangling rodent to take a better look. It was more streamlined in build and had a much more aggressive attitude than any of his former captives. It seemed to challenge its captor. This outlaw would not be imprisoned easily.

The boy moved to the tire prison and dropped the outlaw within, forcing it to join the others. Alas, it would be counted as a regular capture but the latest captive was by far the smallest, in spite of being toughest. Indeed, it was less than half the size of the other mice.

But, what was this?

All the mice scrambled to the edge of their prison, squealing in panic. They seemed to want to get as far away from the new arrival as possible. They were panicked. How could Billy the Kid be so mean as to be upsetting even to fellow outlaws?

The pointed face of the Kid danced from mouse to mouse, evaluating the situation carefully. Then a smile seemed to cross that sharp face and the animal attacked the nearest mouse.

What was happening? The vicious stranger was by far the smallest prisoner yet he attacked with wanton disregard for his well being. It was little wonder that the other prisoners seemed transfixed with fear.

Being soft hearted toward all animals, the boy could not hold his captives and observe the carnage happening before his very gaze. Quickly, he lifted the edge of the tire prison and mice scattered in all directions with Billy the Kid in hot pursuit.

At dinner that evening, the boy related his story to the family. He could not describe the strange mouse in great depth but it was unnecessary. As soon as he began his description of the animal, his elder brother began to laugh.

"Why," commented the brother, "It's no wonder the mice were terrified. What you caught was a shrew. They feast on mice. In fact, the shrew must eat its own weight every few hours."

Now the mystery had finally been solved. The shrew had reacted in glee as he had been dropped smack into the middle of the biggest living banquet he could ever imagine.

And to the mice, he was every bit as dangerous as the infamous Billy the Kid.

NEW YEAR'S DILEMMA

New Year's Eve, 1950, and the family sat around the kitchen table, the only room on the lower floor of the house, and waited for midnight.

The past year hadn't been a prosperous one. Crops had suffered hail damage and the grocery store wanted to be paid, paid for supplies long digested and forgotten.

With money from grain payments yet to arrive, it was time to look forward to a new year. Grain was still lying in bins due to inadequate shipping quotas. Surely there would be better times for the family.

The three brothers and their mother sat at the table, playing games and talking, happily. The light coming from the coal oil lamp on the table was dim. But it was the only source of light, since electricity was not available.

Normally it hung from a hook in ceiling but, due to the game they were playing, a little extra light was needed.

The game progressed nicely. The family loved this game, Monopoly, and could play it for hours. The youngest brother was spoiled though; he would play only if everyone agreed to let him buy Boardwalk and Park Place. The older brothers, both adult, humoured him, as did their mother.

The lamp's light was fading, making it difficult to see. The eldest of the brothers reached over and pulled it toward him. Obviously, the wick was too low. He turned it higher, ignoring the smoke rising above the chimney. Yes, that was the problem. The light grew brighter.

Satisfied with his efforts the boy moved the lamp away, toward the back of the table, nearer the window. Someone pushed it back farther to clear the way for the game, back farther toward the window.

Then it happened! It was sudden! A tiny finger of flame emitted by the over-worked wick reached out, flicking at the curtain which hung by the side of the window and heated it. The curtain burst into flame!

The family jumped to their feet, one of the boys grabbing the burning curtain and tearing it from the window. He threw it to the floor and stomped on it. The flame died, but it was too late. The flames had already caught on the section of curtain which stretched across the top of the window and the end of one decorative, paper streamer, left over from Christmas. The blaze followed the streamer upward and across the ceiling of the room and, soon, the folding paper bell hanging at its centre, began to smoulder.

By now, the entire family was in frantic motion. Three boys and their mother were grasping at burning curtains, burning streamers, tearing them down and throwing them to the floor to be smashed underfoot until they were extinguished and posed no further threat.

The mother stood in the centre of the room, slapping burning material to keep the fire from spreading and burning the entire house to the ground. Just as she turned a backless chair over some burning streamers, the string suspending the paper bell burned through allowing it to fall. On its way to the floor it brushed past the mother's head. As it lay there, the youngest boy grabbed the backless chair and turned it upside down on top of the burning bell. The fire died. Then a shout echoed through the room.

One of the older sons had noticed that, as the bell passed his mother, her hair had started on fire. Thinking quickly, he placed his hand on her head, smothering the flaming hair. All that remained as witness to the near catastrophe was the stench of burning protein.

Feeling that someone had grasped her head, the mother spun and spoke to her son, not realizing her hair had been on fire.

"Stop that!" she said, "Can't you see I'm fighting a fire?"

Moments later, all remnants of the blaze were extinguished.

Only now did the family stop and realize the peril they had faced. Only now did the mother acknowledge that she had been in danger. She finally accepted that her hair had been burning.

The fire had passed and calm began to descend on the group. They returned to their game. The only task remaining being to explain to the absent father the events that had occurred, leading up to the excitement and near disaster.

THE GARDEN

He recalled, while still a child, his father planting the largest garden in the neighbourhood. The plot, approximately one full acre of land, had to be cultivated with a tractor and field implement each spring. Being one of those one might call a "perfectionist," he always had to till the soil in both directions, ensuring that no large clumps remained.

Then the seeding in perfectly straight rows took place. Planned by stretching a length of binder twine between two pegs so that one could follow the string, exactly, with the edge of a hoe, making the trench where each seed would be meticulously planted. Although the distance between types of seeds varied, the distances for any particular seed remained constant from year to year.

His father felt things grew better in straight rows and was concerned with appearance, since anyone driving up the lane had to pass the garden. His methods, however, were tried and true and each year the result was a perfect garden.

It really didn't matter to Ben how fast things grew, as he would merely have to begin hilling potatoes as soon as they were a few inches high. The faster they grew, the sooner he and his siblings would have increased duties.

When the planting was complete, in spite of the cultivation which was to break up the soil and kill any weeds, it was always the weeds that were first to poke their heads through. By the time the vegetables began to grow, they would have already "weeded" the garden at least once.

With the men often busy with farm work or chores, Ben's mother and the children became responsible for the weeding. Since the weeds seemed at times particularly plentiful, the entire family would join in. In a way, these were enjoyable times, as the whole family pulled weeds, hoed, hilled or simply kidded each other. In a manner of speaking, these 'weeding gatherings' became a 'Sunday family day'.

As the days grew longer and spring became summer, the family realized some of the fruits of their labours. Fresh peas, potatoes, carrots and radishes began to appear on the table. No longer did the "spuds" have black or brown spots on them. Instead, they were tiny, round globes, boiled and often served in milk. This was the one time of year that parents had no difficulty persuading their children to eat their vegetables.

When the harvest season approached, it became necessary to pick the vegetables from the garden and either can or store them for the winter.

"Waste not, want not," was the motto of the family. So relatives gathered to choose the vegetables needed to survive the winter.

Ben's younger cousins and he played freely while the adults were at work. Since they did not see each other often, they looked forward to the summer vegetable reaps. The children played Blind Man's Bluff, tag or cowboys and Indians, beginning early in the afternoon and continuing well into the evening. It was usually quite dark when the last of the bounty was stored and ready for transport.

With the completion of the activities of the day, a bon fire was built in the garden and roasting wieners and marshmallows began while the adults visited. Fuel for the fire, often, came from the dried stalks of corn or other plants that had to be burned, so it was decided to carry out this chore at once and enjoy the warmth.

All too soon, the play and other activities would come to an end. Before the family knew it, their guests would depart, taking with them half of the fruit of their labours. Ben always wondered why they didn't simply let their relatives grow the gardens and tend to them throughout the season and then he would visit them to gather the winter's crop. It certainly seemed the easier way to do things, but it never happened.

Once the family had taken what they needed, the neighbours and relatives were invited over. The remainder of the garden was stripped in a single evening as the guests descended on it like buzzards. This was one of the most enjoyable times of year for Ben and his cousins.

It was the memories of the "Great Depression" that created his father's need to feed everyone. When his family had existed on what they could grow, it spurred Ben's parents on to plant excessively. It was during this period that his parents had begun helping the neighbours and relatives and had set the standards by which they continued to live.

Jay Bernard

SUMMER TROUBLE

Grade nine had been a disaster. The year had ended with a track meet and he had tried many events only to fail at each one. It seemed the boy was destined to finish last, be laughed at and ridiculed by fellow students for, "Being so stupid as to try any events, especially the races!"

Now it was summer and he should have forgotten the whole affair, should have enjoyed the warm days and starry nights. But anger burned in his soul. He would show them.

The family was moving to a different town in the fall, and this alone should have helped save his dignity. He was moving away from those who criticized him openly.

For the summer, as the family needed money desperately, his brother-in-law had managed to arrange for the boy to work with his older brother and father on a diamond drill, drilling holes in a cement dam. It seemed strange, and everyone laughed when they were told that he had a summer job drilling holes in a dam. After all, dams were built to hold water and really didn't need any extra holes.

Nonetheless, that is what the job entailed. Cracks appeared within their super structure and to re-enforce them, holes were to be drilled vertically, capped at the bottom and fresh cement forced into them from the top. But it seemed nothing he did made sense.

On the first day of July, he went to the job site with his father and prepared the work the following day. It was strange, at first, being the only teenager living in a camp and always in the presence of grown men with whom he had nothing in common.

"How is the ham radio work going?"

"Have you spoken to any Russians lately?"

"How much did you pay for that new car your driving?"

"So, when is your wedding date?"

Conversations were always beyond the interest or understanding of a sixteen year old. Often, when he did attempt to take part in the conversations, he was rebuked or ignored. They were adult conversations in an adult camp.

Therefore, it became necessary to develop other interests. Fishing! Now that was something that sounded exciting. He heard there were large trout in the river. In fact he had picked fish from tiny pools below the dam where they became stranded as the water subsided.

A new plan was conceived. The next weekend, he bought a fishing rod with money that he had been allowed to keep out of his pay. Normally, he gave his everything to his father as soon as it was signed but he had been offered an allowance.

"If you want to go to high school next fall, you have to let us have your pay, so we can afford it," his father kept saying over and over.

He knew the family had little money so he didn't complain a great deal about giving up his money. And he was grateful for having enough left to purchase the fishing rod.

It was a magnificent rod. Constructed of a bamboo and fitted neatly into a wooden box.

"It's a fly rod." he was told.

"That's nice. Now we know what kind of rod it is," he thought, as he attached a Len Thompson spoon to the line.

Cast as he might, he could not attract a fish. He added a J-hook and worm and fitted a float to the line to allow it to sit in the water, still no luck. He reeled in the entire mess and laid it on the dam in disgust. He'd never catch a fish. This whole idea had been a mistake!

His father picked up the gear, looked at it carefully and cast into the still water, held back by the dam, and relaxed. Moments later, the rod bent and the man had a fight on his hands. It had to be a big one. Look at the way it fights! When it was landed, it was, indeed, a magnificent fish.

"See," said his father. "You just have to be patient."

He picked up the rod and cast into the water, emulating every move his father had made. Two hours later, no fish had been curious enough to take the hook. He reeled the line in and set the fishing gear down, this time for good.

Other plans had to be made to pass the hours of the dreary summer days when he was not working. Finally there seemed to be a solution as one of the younger men in camp mentioned there were tennis courts nearby and that his normal partner was otherwise occupied.

"Do you know how to play tennis?" he asked.

"No," came the reply, "But I'd love to learn".

The tennis adventure turned out to be nearly as exciting as fishing. The ball moved too quickly and was impossible to hit. When he did hit it, there was no way to tell which direction it would travel.

Somewhat disgruntled at his success rate with new endeavours, the boy decided to occupy himself in an attempt to perfect or improve something with which he was already familiar, hopefully something that required no equipment. He would run.

Perhaps he could learn to run faster and gain acceptance more readily in his new school next fall. Besides, if he qualified for the divisional track meet, he would run against those who had laughed at his attempts in the past. Yes! He would learn to run!

Each morning for the next week, he rose and went running before breakfast was served in the camp. He timed himself and each day attempted to shorten the time set the day before. It seemed to be no use. Regardless of what he did, he could not decrease the times for his runs.

His first reaction was to simply give up and chart it up as one more failed effort. But the desire for retaliation against those who had found him a source of humour reappeared and spurred him on. There must be some solution.

Perhaps his father would allow him to drive the family car, an old nineteen fifty Dodge. He had taken lessons from an older brother and was quite proficient as a driver. He asked, and much to his surprise, was granted permission to drive the vehicle on any of the roads in camp, although he was cautioned, "Be careful."

At first, driving the old car to and fro, throughout the camp, seemed to fulfill his needs but, after very few days it too became boring. He was still possessed by the idea that he could learn to run faster if only he could develop a suitable training method.

Then the idea struck! Of course! Why hadn't he thought of it before?

He could put the car in gear, start it moving down the trail and, while holding the steering wheel in one hand and the door ledge with other, run along beside it. He did not think this would be considered dangerous because, when the car's speed increased to the point that he had difficulty keeping up, he would merely jump into the driver's seat and put the brakes on. After a slight rest, he could repeat the procedure. He had the answer at last. And he could watch the speedometer to see how fast he really was running.

The boy not only attempted to carry out his plan, but he found it to be highly successful. Each day, he allowed the speedometer to register a greater speed before jumping into the driver's seat. Each day he would go faster. It was working!

When September arrived, he began grade ten in the new school and, much to his delight, learned that the annual track meet would be held in the fall. If the training had been successful he would do well in try outs. He won! He was the fastest in his age group in the entire school! Going on to the divisional meet, he ran the shorter sprints and anchor for the schools' relay team and won two of the events against his old school mates.

He felt vindicated! He had proven his ability! It had been hard work but it had been worth it. He had won!

Nobody was laughing at him now!

And nor would his father laugh if he ever discovered his car had nearly rolled into the dam during training.

MONKEY SEE!
MONKEY DO!

Dating back to his boyhood, one could see that Ben had always been a lover of unusual pets. He had owned the average variety of pet, but the most notable pets, as he was growing up, consisted of magpies, sea gulls, frogs, snakes, turkeys, ducks and pigs. These were, indeed, not the type of pets one expected to discover following a young farm boy around the yard. But they were the desired friends of the young lad.

Growing into adulthood, did little to change his desires. He still dwelt on the unusual animal as a pet and companion. Whenever someone came along, holding an animal which was out of the ordinary, he was impressed. When he sighted a lady with a pet porcupine, he wanted one. When he met someone leading a Margay, Ocelot or some other form of exotic cat through a park, he wanted one. Therefore, it was only natural that, when he came across a young man with a Woolly Monkey, his affection turned to this other pet.

The animal was fascinating. Its master entered restaurants, sat and ordered tea and, before drinking any, produced a miniature cup for his furry companion and filled it.

The entire performance was a spectacle which grabbed the interest of any bystander. However, with the exception of Ben, the most interested onlookers were, inevitably, ladies, who the little monkey did not appreciate, for some unknown reason.

Over a week passed, with Ben admiring the monkey on a daily basis and becoming more and more enthralled with the little fellow. Then it happened!

While walking through a downtown department store, Ben noticed a large red sign with black letters. It simply jumped out at him! "MONKEY FOR SALE" read the sign, "$50.00 (50% off regular price)".

Ben could not let an opportunity of this magnitude go unchecked.

"What species of monkey is for sale?" he asked the nearest clerk.

"A Squirrel Monkey," the clerk replied.

"Could I see it?" asked Ben.

The clerk walked a few paces and stood beside a cage, housing a brown coloured animal. It was such a cute little fellow that there was no alternative, it was to be his to own and to love.

"I'll take him!" said Ben and produced the fifty dollars indicated on the sign.

Clutching his prize, in the tiny cage, the young man left the store and returned to his car. He could hardly wait to tell his friends and introduce his roommate to their new companion. Putting the car in gear, he drove home and began to call friends. They arrived shortly and were quite amused as they observed the little fellow.

Then a problem erupted.

"Where will you keep him?" asked one friend, "That cage is far too small."

He was, of course correct. Some adjustment had to be made.

Ben returned downtown to get some fencing material made of small mesh with which he hoped to construct a cage. It was not a difficult job and, before he knew it, the monkey's new accommodation was complete. Measuring approximately one metre square, and having two perches neatly located within, it would be the perfect home for his new pet. He picked up the tiny cage, placed its opening facing that of the new, larger enclosure and encouraged the little monkey to enter it.

In no time at all, the little fellow had leaped into his new abode and, once he had discovered the food which had been left for him, he made himself right at home. This was the largest play area the little fellow had seen for some time, if not the largest ever. He ate; he drank and swung from perch to perch. Life was good!

Whenever guests would come by, the monkey was the centre of attention. As unbelievable as it seemed, one could toss three grapes at the little fellow, simultaneously, and he would catch all three. He grasped the first two, one in each hand, rapidly transferred the one in his right hand to his mouth with lightning fast dexterity, and caught the third before it landed on the floor of the cage. Unfortunately, the monkey's amusement seemed to last only until its appetite was filled, and then he refused to take any further part in the game. Guests, however, continued to stare at him, waiting for other interesting activities to begin.

The little monkey would soon become bored with these observations and developed a behaviour which would certainly break his boredom and amuse the visitors.

While sitting on the higher of the two perches, he calmly looked at himself, aimed, and began a contest of one to determine who could urinate the farthest. He developed a range far greater than that afforded by his cage and soon had little puddles on the floor, even managing to develop an aim which was quite accurate and, certainly surprising to any onlooker who may venture too close.

A few days later, another problem developed. Returning home from work, Ben noticed the cage was empty. Where in the world had his monkey disappeared to? Every cupboard door in the apartment was open and broken dishes lay on the floor. And there, feet braced against the fridge door, little hands grasping the handle, was the monkey. He had learned to open doors by observation, practiced on the cupboards and was now advancing into the big leagues by attempting to open the door, behind which, his grapes would be found.

Some changes needed to be made, most notably to the method of locking the cage. A new lock was constructed which, although no more intricate in its operation, would require greater strength than that of a monkey in order to open.

Once escaped from his cage, however, it was extremely difficult to persuade the little creature to return. Being far more intelligent than any of the farm animals with which Ben had grown up, an entirely new experience awaited.

"Corner the thing!" yelled his room mate.

It was no use. The monkey headed for the bedroom and scurried under the bed. If Ben moved left, the monkey moved right, if he moved up, the monkey went down, always moving in the opposite direction and always keeping the bed between the pursuer and the pursued. Only after a trail of grapes leading to the cage door, could the little primate be lured back into captivity.

Once realizing its alluring possibilities, food became both the tool utilized to return the animal to its cage and the key to ever lengthening periods of freedom. A string was stretched across the living room from one corner to the other, passing close to the window. Owner and guests alike would be totally enthralled by the little fellow's ability to cross the room walking on the string. Reaching the end of the rope, he would calmly reverse directions and traverse the room again.

On one occasion, however, the monkey was walking his tight rope when a new method of convincing the imp to return to his cage was discovered. Halfway across the room, the little fellow chanced to glance at the window and there, staring intently at the monkey's antics, was the neighbour's Persian cat. To the little monkey the cat was an ominous beast. Immediately, the monkey emitted an ear shattering scream, dropped to the floor, dashed inside its cage and sat on the highest perch while continuing to scream at the invader.

As days passed, an unfamiliar, pungent odour began to fill the apartment. The monkey's cage was cleaned daily, the pools were wiped from the floor, but, in spite of Ben's efforts, the repulsive odour remained. There was only one course of action remaining. The beast would have to be bathed.

Picking up a towel, Ben reached into the cage and captured the elusive little creature and wrapped it in folds of the towel with only its tiny head protruding. To the bathroom and into the waiting tub, went the monkey, screaming and scratching all the way. Several bites later, the monkey was bathed.

The most notable development in this whole affair was perhaps the relationship which existed between the monkey and the two room mates. Ben attempted to develop the same type of relationship with his monkey that he had noted existing between his friend and the Woolly monkey. The more effort he put in, however, the more distant the monkey seemed to grow. Yet, it did develop quite a close bond with Ben's room mate; and, this in spite of, or perhaps because of, the roommate's cold attitude. The more efforts Ben made to convince his pet to become buddies, the closer his roommate and the monkey became. Finally, with the room mate developing no affection for the little beast and Ben totally disgruntled, an ad was placed in the local newspaper.

"Monkey for Sale!" it read, "Good deal! Only one hundred dollars"

No responses came. The following edition began in a similar manner but the price had dropped to fifty dollars. Perhaps, he could at least regain his initial investment, thought Ben.

Still there was no response.

The next week, the ad read, "Free Monkey! Available to persons wishing to supply a unique pet with love and a good home"

Fortunately, Ben's sister-in-law came by with a young niece who was quite preoccupied with the tiny beast.

"Yes," Ben assured the girl and her mother, "this would be a fine pet and could live right in the little girl's bedroom."

Off to its new residence went the monkey, quite content with its new owner and his bedroom accommodation. Within days, however, the monkey paradise was lost. The little girl was allergic to the animal and disgusted by its smell. Her new pet was moved to the bedroom of her older brother.

Two days later, the local newspaper carried an ad, placed by the brother. "Monkey, cage and accessories, FREE to a good home!"

Jay Bernard

SEX EDUCATION
FOR THE FARM BOY

Today, sex education is conducted in the school to assist parents in this touchy subject. However, this has not always been the case.

Traditionally, sex education of young people was not nearly as sophisticated as it is today. Farm children learned about sex in a variety of ways. It could happen when working with farm animals and observing their activities. In some cases older brothers and sisters or even their older cousins, as was often the case, took charge of this form of vital education.

Parents were often too self conscious, when it came to discussing sex and sexual relations between people to have any meaningful discussion with their children. Perhaps this is because they were not totally clear on the functions of their own bodies or, it was due to an ingrained Victorian attitude. Whatever the reason, not many parents were open with their children and very few carried on any type of discussion on such a taboo topic. Guidelines for the do's and don'ts of sex were not offered.

One boy came to school in junior high school laughing. When asked what was so funny, he replied, "Dad and I had a talk about the birds and the bees last night."

"Why is that funny?" Ben asked.

"Well," he replied, "Dad took me into the living room and asked how much I knew about sex. So I explained. After a few minutes he excused himself and left."

But, when all else failed, there was always a doctor's book in the community. It was never published for this particular learning purpose. Instead, it was meant as a guide to curing all types of ailments in a rural community where doctors were scarce or some distance away. Whatever its purpose, it sufficed when it came to a lesson in human anatomy which was often conducted in secret out behind the barn.

Ben asked his mother where babies came from when he was around ten or eleven years of age. Being a very reserved woman she found the subject somewhat difficult but she did not insult his intelligence by telling him he had been found under a cabbage or the stork brought him. She didn't even mention that he was found in the hospital. Instead she attempted to outline the truth as briefly as possible without going into the gory details.

Knowing there was no way to avoid the issue; she looked at him and said, "Do you know where eggs come from?"

Without thinking, Ben said, "Yes."

Because he, like so many farm lads, gathered them every single day he knew eggs came from chickens.

"Well," said his mother, "Babies come from the same place!"

Not wanting to appear completely stupid, Ben failed to ask for clarification of her response. Indeed, he merely allowed her to think she had cleared up all confusion and dropped the subject.

At that tender age, however, he was not aware of the fact that chickens could actually carry on a relationship, which resulted in fertile eggs.

He was certainly glad that he had occasion to research the issue further as he grew older. Had he accepted the explanation offered by his mother, life could have been very different.

Who wants to go through life thinking they'd been laid by a chicken?

THE HUNT IS ON

Snipe! Every meal for the past week, the conversation at the dinner table at the old boarding house had revolved around snipe. Set in motion by Matt and Ben, who had grown up hunting and an agreement by the cook to "fix 'em up nice" the thought of bagging a few birds proved enthralling to the city types at the table, especially Fisher.

Matt and Ben hunted often and Fisher, who liked to be known simply as "The Fish" bothered them constantly about taking him along. He had never hunted or handled a gun but had a strong urge to "just kill something" and be part of the gang. So to a large extent, the snipe hunting talk was for the benefit of The Fish.

Due to his constant begging, the two farm boys had taken Fisher out before, in an attempt to offer some instruction on the proper use of a firearm. However, the entire outing had bordered on disaster. Teaching him to aim, fire and hit a target had not been too much trouble, as The Fish seemed to have a natural eye, but his concentration proved lacking.

While holding a loaded rifle and aiming at his target the new recruit waved the firearm around dangerously. This resulted in a last minute instruction to ensure the safety of fellow hunters.

"Hey Fish," Ben said as his student was about to fire at his target. "Just one more thing, hold that gun still and never aim it at anybody."

"What?" replied Fisher as he twisted around to ensure he had heard the instruction correctly.

Ben had found himself looking at the business end of the rifle and struggling with an adrenalin flow in his body. He knew what the rifle could do and had certainly never intended to be subjected to this situation.

"Aim it away," he managed to stutter.

The gun didn't move. Fortunately, Matt managed to gently move the gun aside and remove it from Fisher's grasp. Thus ended the lesson and, Ben and Matt hoped, any urge by their friend to pursue their chosen pastime.

But it hadn't stopped The Fish's enthusiasm for hunting. If anything, the nagging had gotten worse as he demanded to be taken on a hunt. Thus, the reason for the talk of snipe; this, the would-be hunter was assured, would be a special hunt, just for him, and was a great way to get into the sport. Most country boys had been on snipe hunts and now it was his turn.

When the weekend rolled around, the snipe talk increased.

"Tonight we'll go," Fisher was assured. "Get some sleep today because we have to go after dark."

At midnight the three loaded into a car and headed for a stream twelve miles out of town.

"Where are the guns?" Fisher asked.

He was assured that there was no need for firearms on this hunt. And it was a great way to get him into the sport since his history with guns had been less than satisfactory.

"If you get too excited, we might have an accident and somebody could get hurt if we have guns," Matt assured him. "So we'll do it this way first, then when you're calmer, we'll get into the guns."

"How are we going to get anything without guns?" Fisher asked. "Are they just going to come to us?"

"Exactly!" replied Matt. "We'll catch them alive and wring their necks. It will all be worthwhile when you taste 'em."

Ben and Matt explained how animals are attracted to light and that would be the key. The birds would, indeed, come to the hunters.

Fortunately, several animals were passed on the road and each seemed attracted to the car's headlights, a fact the experienced hunters were quick to point out. Suddenly, the hunting technique made perfect sense to the rookie.

Upon their arrival at the designated hunting grounds, the three young men crawled out of the vehicle and Matt pulled a flashlight and large bag out of the trunk.

"C'mon," He said. "Let's get down to the water."

Upon reaching their destination, Matt handed Fisher the flashlight and bag.

"Here," he said. "Since you're new at this, you get the easy job. Just sit here and hold the bag wide open with the flashlight behind it. Ben and I'll head up the creek and flush up some snipe. Remember you have to be perfectly quiet and sit still."

With final instructions given, the snipe flushers headed upstream for fifty yards before cutting off, back to the car. Chuckling a little, they hopped in and headed back to their beds and a good night's sleep, leaving their friend waiting for snipes.

With the arrival of morning, a breakfast out seemed a fine way to start the day to Matt and Ben. As they emerged through the front gate a pitiful sight awaited. Up the street came a very bedraggled, wet Fisher, a flashlight in one hand and a bag dragging along, its top held tightly in the other. And he was in no mood to talk about hunting, or anything else for that matter.

Fisher had been had and he new it. And hunting became a subject never to be discussed again at the dinner.

HALLOWEEN FIASCO

He begged! He pleaded! No matter what Ben did, he could not convince his brother to loan him a car for Halloween.

It was a terrible disappointment for him. Ben had promised Gord, Jerry and Larry that he would borrow a car and they would go Haloweening in the country. They didn't plan to cause any real trouble, just a few practical jokes with nothing hurt or damaged. However, everything had fallen through. His father had issued a flat "No!" and refused to even discuss the matter. So he had attempted to save some face by borrowing his brother's car. The result was the same.

Ben called his friend Jerry to break the bad news and found it very embarrassing. Jerry announced that he had permission to take his family's car.

"Okay! So now we'll make plans."

Promptly at eight o'clock, the boys met at the local restaurant and sat in a booth near the back. After a brief discussion, they determined the best plan of attack would be to visit Ben's uncle's farm and pick up a few bales. They climbed into the old Dodge, Jerry behind the wheel, and headed out of town, chuckling happily as they made their way over the gravel roads.

Twenty minutes later, they stopped the old car to talk. They planned to turn off the headlights and move as close as possible to the buildings, park behind a clump of trees and complete their journey on foot. It would mean moving quietly along the ditch.

They parked the car, jumped off the approach into the ditch and headed for the farm yard. As they neared the yard, the boys crouched even lower and then, suddenly, they heard it. A starter whirred, a motor caught and headlights pierced the blackness of the night.

The headlights began to form a circular pattern in the darkness, coming closer and closer to where the boys sat, huddled in the ditch. Then they saw it! Someone, holding a rifle, was sitting on the hood of the car as it came through the field! Still, the boys were sure they were not in any real danger. This had to be one of Ben's cousins.

Boom! A shot broke through the stillness of the night, then again and a third! The boys began to beat a quick retreat as quietly as they could. Dropping to their hands and knees, they crawled along the grassy bottom of the ditch, keeping the grade of the road above them to avoid being seen from the ever circling car. Several more shots were heard from the rifle as the boys continued to crawl back to where their car waited.

Frightened, they crawled nearly a half mile before they dared to stand and look around. Headlights still circled in the field but were now a safe distance away. The boys then broke into a run, heading for the trees as fast as they possibly could.

Once seated in the safety of their car, they discussed the situation earnestly. They had planned no damage but a challenge had been issued. They were cold, their hands were sore and their knees were cramped from crawling along the ditch. It was unforgivable. Someone had to pay for this!

"Well, for one thing," said Ben, "My uncle's whole family has always bragged that no one could upset their toilets. Tonight we have to find out…"

"…Let's go over to my cousin's place," Ben added decisively.

Putting their car in motion, it took little time to arrive at a corner, close to the scene of the upcoming crime. With the car parked they walked toward their victim's house. Slowly, ever so slowly, they neared their destination. Yes, there it was – the out house, about twenty yards from the main house. They approached it, walking boldly up to the small, square building, took it by its four corners and carefully lifted it.

But since they didn't want to upset it or make any noise; they simply moved it back, off the hole so carefully dug beneath it. For a brief moment, Jerry's foot slipped and he nearly tumbled into the man made crevice, regaining his footing in the nick of time.

"Close," he mumbled with obvious relief in his voice.

Moving carefully into a thicket behind the toilet, it was time for a disturbance to begin. Discussion of upsetting the little house became louder and the boys began to move grass and shrubs, making just enough noise to attract attention.

A door had opened! The faint squeak was obvious. And a stealthy figure was making its way toward them, progressing quietly in the shadow of the house to avoid detection.

As the figure neared the corner of the house Gord shouted, "Run!", and off went the boys, heading into the trees.

"Stop," shouted a man's voice. "Get back here. You can't fool around with me. Leave my toilet alooooonnnne!"

And the shadow dropped out of sight.

REVENGE

With the sudden disappearance of their pursuer, the night took a turn for the better. At last, the boys were not on the losing end. They had taken a huge step forward on their path to revenge, after being forced to crawl on hand and knee along a ditch.

But the night was still young. There was much to be done before dawn broke and ghouls and goblins disappeared for another year.

They drove, slowly, back toward their earlier target, lights off, keeping the car's engine as quiet as possible. They parked amid a friendly grove of trees where they had left the car earlier and waited. Houselights were turned off and yet they waited. This time, there would be no mistake, no encounter. By the time they began to move along the ditch (again), they were certain everyone would expect Halloweeners to have gone home long ago. Their luck held. No one challenged them thus far.

As they quietly crept alongside a row of carriganas that formed a ring around the yard, Jerry noticed a coil of rope lying on the ground.

"Hey, look at this," he whispered to his companions. "Do you think we could find a use for this?"

"You betcha!" replied Ben. "It's really long. Let's tie it around the outhouse and tie it to my uncle's truck." The others agreed.

Carefully, they looped the rope around the toilet before Gord slipped quietly through the trees and tied the loose end to the rear bumper of a pick-up. With the stage set, the boys retraced their steps to the safety of their car.

"We're set," said Ben. "But they'll see the rope in the morning. They have to drive that truck now!"

To ensure the success of their plan, some daring was needed. Driving into the farm yard quietly the car's headlights were flicked on. Cranking the steering wheel hard to the left and flooring the accelerator was enough to shatter the stillness that had fallen on the night. The car's rear end spun around, spraying rocks through tree rows, against the pump house, against the house, making a terrific clatter.

A light appeared in the house and a shadowy figure burst through the front door.

As the man jumped into the truck and started the motor, the boys circled the ground once more and headed for an exit. The car sped away, the headlights focusing on another shape moving toward the trees, then seeming to vanish. The truck headed for the road, dragging a long rope behind it, but what had been a toilet, lay in ruins, nestled in the trees.

"Yes!" Ben yelled. "That'l teach them to fool with us."

"Look out!" Jerry yelled.

Their confidence instantly hit bottom as the events took yet, another unforeseen twist. The truck was gaining and a second set of headlights were coming at them rapidly.

All they could think of was. "Maybe if we reach the highway, we can outdistance them."

The car darted down the road and onto the main highway. This highway idea was a mistake! Now the truck was right beside them.

"Get off the main road," shouted Ben. "Turn into that town."

Gord spun the wheel and turned into the street. Around the block they went.

"Can't you lose them?" Jerry shouted.

"No can do," Gord replied. "I think the gear shift linkage just broke. We're stuck in second gear."

At these words, the car came up to a stop sign, the truck right behind them. There was no where to go. Their path was blocked on both sides by the other vehicles and there, directly in front of their car, sitting crosswise on the road, was a police cruiser. The boys could only think of locking the doors, barricading themselves in the car, and holding the fort.

With the farmers pounding on the doors on one side of the car, and police approaching from the other, there seemed to be only one safe choice left – the police.

Not that being arrested was meeting with anyone's approval but it certainly seemed the better of the two options the boys were offered. They sure didn't want to step out of the car and into the hands of three, very large, very angry farmers. Picking the lesser of two evils, the young criminals stepped out and were ushered unceremoniously into the back of the police car.

The next stop was the town jail, a single cell already crowded to the limit.

"Welcome home boys, and happy Halloween," said a man with corporal stripes on his sleeve. "It's not the best hotel in town, but for tonight, it'll be home for you!"

Jay Bernard

HILLBILLYITIS

If anything was ever a certainty, it was that Jake was a hillbilly in every aspect of his life. He dressed like a hillbilly, walked like a hillbilly and, in general, lived like a hillbilly; living alone in what proved to be little more than a granary tucked away among the trees.

Company rarely disrupted the day for Jake but, when it did, they were welcomed with open arms and a hot pot of tea or some of the "stuff" the neighbours claimed, he, "brewed up hisself", was available.

Upon being invited to a local wedding, Jake was more than happy to take part and he dressed his best for the occasion. There he sat while the ceremony was taking place, plaid shirt, coveralls and tie. But it was his best tie, albeit his only one, and coveralls and shirt had been freshly washed.

Like many individuals considered "different" by the community, Jake had his talents and his drawbacks. If 'it' had strings or a bow could be used, he could pick it up and make beautiful music. As a result, the community, urged him to start a band and this met with his favour. Several community members joined him to form the group. Then it was decided they would need uniforms and that they would perform locally.

Jake's drawback was that when he became nervous, he stuttered. Therefore, his position in the band would not include performing vocals.

Uniforms were ordered from the catalogue and arrived just in time for the band's first performance. It was outstanding. The musicians looked professional and sounded professional, much to the joy of the dancers who clogged away the night. In fact, the social affair was so successful, the band was asked to perform again the following weekend.

Wanting to be as stunning as they had been in their first outing, uniforms required cleaning and were gathered by a band member who agreed to take them the twenty miles to town, have them dry cleaned and return them for the next performance – all of the uniforms except one that is. Jake decided it would be far less expensive to take care of the cleaning himself. He did. He took his uniform home and promptly washed it.

When the following weekend rolled around, the band took to the stage only to notice their leader was missing. Just before the first number was to be played, good ol' Jake appeared, jacket sleeves up to his elbows and pant legs up to his knees. The suit had shrunk badly. But the worst was yet to come. As Jake bent to pick up his instrument, an ominous ripping sound thundered through the auditorium. For the remainder of the night, Jack sat while he played.

Although seldom venturing into town except when in need of groceries, Jake did own a car, a 1930 Ford of which he was very proud. Before each outing the car was washed down by the creek.

One morning friends arrived at Jake's shack shortly after breakfast to announce a tragedy. Their car had broken down and their elderly father had passed away in the night. If possible, they needed someone to transport the body to the undertaker and Jake was elected. Being a neighbourly sort of a guy and always ready to help, he agreed.

The Ford was washed, started and made it's way to the neighbour's, the body was laid carefully on the back seat, Jake and two neighbours climbed into the front seat and they were off to the mortuary.

All went smoothly until they neared town. At that point, a police officer noticed that the car seemed to be swerving its way down main-street uncontrollably. The swerving was the result of attempts to avert potholes on the road, but the officer thought it could be the result of drinking. He pulled the Ford over and approached the vehicle.

"You boys been drinking?" the policeman asked.

His approach and the body in the back seat made Jake very, very nervous.

"N...N...N...No, o....o...officer," Jake replied. "W...W...W... We're fine."

With that the lawman looked into the back seat at the sprawled figure of a man.

"What about him?" he asked.

"Du-Du- Don't worry 'bout him, o-o-o-officer," stuttered Jake. "H-H-H-He's dead!"

With those words, Jake and the boys found themselves with a police escort into town.

MONTEZUMA'S REVENGE REVISITED

He deserved a holiday in California and had waited long and dreamed of the day of departure. Finally, it was reality.

Ok, let's take a quick trip on Montezuma's Revenge. Close your eyes and imagine a piece of yellow steel rising about ten or twelve stories above the ground. It's curved upward and little more than a hollow tube which has a single railed track.

Now crawl into a little roller coaster-style car, pull down the shoulder restraining harness and get ready.

And you're off! The acceleration is unbelievable as the car thrusts forward. By the time you've begun to rise, you're already pulling more than three G's and still accelerating. Once you hit the top, for a brief second you sit still, staring straight up into the clouds.

Then it's backwards to do a similar trip up a second rise. Try to hold your arms straight up and catch the wind on the way down. Why not? It might be neat.

Your arms pull backwards with the upper section touching the seat beside your head. It can't be done! And you can't get them to come forward again until you stop.

And the question many ask is, "Why do they call it Montezuma's Revenge."

Yeah right!

Splash Mountain, however, is nothing the same. One enters a floating little boat with no seatbelts whatever. It's sure to be a pleasant trip. The exact opposite of what was just described, and it is. In fact, it is a trip back through the time to your childhood.

What can be more peaceful than floating quietly along listening to soft music and watching mechanically animated characters from Uncle Remus? Hey! We grew up on that stuff and loved it.

It's pleasant! The coloring, the cool inside of the cave like structure after the heat of the stubborn California sun is both relaxing and healing to the soul.

Then that darn Raven has to get into the act!

At first, you don't notice him because his voice is calm and quiet as he softly calls softly, "Go back."

Then he becomes more demanding as he begins to insist, "Go back."

Yeah Right! Here we are in a boat, in ten feet of water, tied to a chain at the bottom and some dumb Raven is calling, "Go back!"

Can't be done, so even though he's beginning to get to you, you put it out of your head – and there he is! Right above your safe little boat!

"It's too late!" he says. "I warned you."

And before you know it, you're being pulled up and up and up by that darn chain that you'd forgotten was tied to your boat.

As you reach the top, it's dry. The water has been left behind and you're in dry dock. A pair of gates open, you sway for a moment, and then your boat tips.

There below you, some five stories, is a pool of water that you are about to slide down a very steep slide and land in.

For an experience like that, there is only one ending. And a lot of it is because your mind is still in Uncle Remus space when you're suddenly jolted back to reality. But I think I summed the whole thing up pretty well the first time I was on it.

As I began to accelerate and my butt left the seat about four inches, I grabbed on to the hand bars beside me with one single little comment. "Holy shit!!!!!!!"

SURPRISE

It was frightening!

No, not frightening – terrifying! The neatly dressed couple had no more than entered the car and settled in their seats when the driver turned, handed them each a white sock and issued an order.

"Put them on – over your eyes! Be sure you can't see!" he said in a nervous tone.

It was easy to see that this was new business for the driver. His hard breathing gave away his excitement. Obviously, he was venturing down a different road in life, far removed from his normal daily routine.

With the blindfolds in place, the car started to slowly back out of the drive. The blindfolded couple could feel it move forward, turning left, right, stopping and then resuming its journey.

The couple knew something different was about to happen as they changed into their clothes for a night on the town to celebrate their anniversary but were not prepared for this. They had barely changed when the tall young man herded them into their own automobile, instructed them where to sit and offered the white socks as blindfolds. Now they were riding through town, away from their home on an indeterminate journey.

The car followed the road around a curve, then another before beginning to accelerate. Obviously, the young driver was intent on following a route unfamiliar to the blindfolded pair. He didn't want to give the slightest inclination as to their whereabouts or their destination.

Finally the car slowed and took a sharp turn to the right, left and right once more. All thoughts as to where they were taken escaped them as the couple soon realized they had completely lost their bearing under their blindfolds. Rather than clinging to the hope of remembering the route, they freed their minds and began to ponder upon their predicament.

The car came to a stop. They must have reached their destination. Where were they? They could only guess!

The vehicle placed in park, their captor instructed them to keep their blindfolds in place as he emerged from the car. While they sat quietly, nervously, in their seat, they heard the trunk open and, after a moment; slam shut.

What had they gotten themselves into? Why hadn't they attempted to run at the first suggestion of being blindfolded? It was too late to contemplate any such actions designed to escape their desperate situation now.

The driver's door opened and a strange voice spoke.

"Don't be alarmed," it said. "I just have to move the car a bit."

The stranger's presence offered little in the way of reassurance. It only added more confusion to the couple's troubled minds. At least they had, in part, been familiar with the original driver – but this was something far different.

The car backed out of a parking stall, moved ahead and then the driver slammed on the brakes, thrusting the occupants forward in their seat. The sound of another auto passing clarified the situation. That had been close!

Once again the car moved forward for a few moments, took several turns and glided to a stop.

"Please stay where you are and keep the blindfolds in place," the strange driver instructed.

The door opened and he departed. A few moments passed and the strange voice reappeared.

"Don't be frightened," he said once again. "I just have to move the car forward a little bit."

What did all this shunting and moving mean? What was in store for the couple? They had changed, light hearted, smiling, excited and on their way to celebrate. Now everything had changed.

The passenger door opened and the voice of the first driver came to them, calm and clear for the first time.

"Alright," he said, "take my hand and get out of the car. Don't take those blindfolds off!"

A few steps and the man stumbled over what, he supposed, was a curb.

"Just keep going straight ahead," instructed their captor.

He placed his hands on the couple's shoulders and guided them through a passageway. They sensed that they were surrounded by people and then they heard low, discrete laughter as they passed through what they supposed to be a large room.

"Stop!" ordered their captor.

Moments later, the three entered what seemed to be an elevator and began to rise. Where could he possibly be taking them? Now they were in a passageway. It was a dark passageway as the absence of light was easy to notice even though their eyes were covered.

"It's dark," said the man. "Where are you taking us? Are we there yet?" "No!" replied their captor. "Just keep walking!"

As the couple moved through the dark maze, fear began to overtake them. Yet it was still somewhat exciting as they heard the breathing of the boy who controlled them begin to quicken.

Passing through another doorway, the sound of water, running water, like a waterfall, reached their ears. And, yes, another strange noise. Perhaps it was the wind on a very high roof top.

"Stop!" their captor ordered once again. "Okay, now you can take off the blindfolds."

As the socks were removed from their eyes the light struck them. It took a moment to focus after wearing blindfolds for so long. But as their eyes regained their vision, they saw IT!

It was amazing! It was unbelievable!

The three were standing in the entry way to the honeymoon suite in the most luxurious room they had ever seen.

In front of them was a large bed and a tiny waterfall sat in the corner.

"Happy anniversary!" their son said, smiling down at them. "I'll pick you up in the morning. Have fun!"

As their son turned to call room service for complimentary beverages, the whole plot finally came into focus in the minds of the kidnapped couple – his parents.

This was their anniversary present. And it was marvellous.

"Thanks, son," they said. "This is wonderful!"

GUNFIGHT AT THE 'OK BACKSTOP'

They had played cowboys and Indians and worked over many an outlaw while they were children. But now, they were no longer children. In fact, they were fully grown adults, and school teachers to boot. But they saw no reason to let that stand in their way; after all, where better than a school track-meet to exhibit their physical skills. And in this case, it meant the fastest draw in the west as exhibited with starter's pistols. They were noisy and really quite harmless but it would create the perfect opportunity to add some distraction from the heat as a group of students waited for their turn at the shot put.

Most everyone has heard of the infamous gunfight at the O.K. Corral, where the Earp brothers and Doc Holiday gunned down an ornery gang of outlaws. However, how many have heard of the gunfight at the O.K. Backstop in the frontier town of Namao? Not many, I think!

Yes, this soon to be famous, gunfight occurred at the nineteen hundred, ninety one, Namao School track meet. It would have happened at a corral, but Namao School doesn't have a proper corral. Therefore, the backstop had to serve the purpose.

All the action took place at about two thirty in the afternoon, as Ricochet Rear advanced on a wild group of outlaws known as the Twelve Year Old Boys Gang who were congregating near the old Back Stop, presently being used for a discuss throwing event.

Now, it must be explained that Ricochet had no evil intent in mind but merely wished to check the action as he approached but, Killer Krupa, the leader of those notorious twelve year olds, had other plans in mind.

"Hey! Ricochet!" he shouted "How about a little shoot-out?"

"Well," responded Ricochet, "It wasn't really in my plans but OK. Where's your gun?" "Minor problem," said Killer Krupa, "Just loan me one of yours."

Now since Ricochet was a nice, congenial fellow, he agreed and tossed the Killer a nine shot, twenty two calibre revolver. For himself, he kept a lesser weapon, a measly five shot thirty eight.

The stage was set! The beady-eyed Krupa peered at our hero, little Ricochet, and said, "Whenever your ready, Sucker!"

Being at a dreadful disadvantage, having only five shots to the Killer's nine did not affect our hero. Undaunted by the staggering odds, Ricochet said, "If you're ready, say go."

"GO!" shouted Killer Krupa and pulled his gun with a lightning fast move.

"Click." went the gun.

Ricochet had pulled his thirty eight and fired. "Barooom!" went the thirty eight.

"Gotcha!" he said.

The Killer couldn't believe either his eyes or ears. He had lost!

"That's not a fair fight," he said, "Let's try that again!"

Keeping with his pleasant nature, Ricochet Rear adjusted his white hat, smiled at the sun and said, "O.K. fine,"

Again they drew! Again the Killer's gun went click! Again he was blown away by Ricochet's thirty eight.

Killer Krupa looked at his gun, "Something seems wrong here," he said as he wiped at the beads of perspiration that gathered under the band of his dirty black hat. He leered at his opponent and said, "We've drawn twice and you've beaten me because my gun keeps going "Click" are you sure there's any bullets in this gun?"

"Well," replied Ricochet, "I'll tell ya somethin'. I may be nice but I'm not stupid. Do you really think I'd give a loaded gun to a guy who was planin' to have a shoot-out with me?"

Now this really seemed to upset Killer Krupa. He became adamant, agitated and almost irrational. "Come on," he said, "Give me some bullets."

Since Ricochet was an understanding and, unusually, fair fellow, not to mention frightened half to death by the Killer's attitude, he agreed.

Trying to be as fair as Ricochet, the Killer agreed to let a bystander say go before they drew their weapons the next time.

"GO!" shouted a voice.

"Barrooom!" Once again Ricochet's pistol fired first. Down went Killer Krupa, finally biting the dust. He had been beaten – fair-and-square, by our hero, three times in a row. Would he ever return to fight again? I wonder.

Mr Helmut Kramer
2678 272B St
Aldergrove BC V4W 3K

Printed in the United States
32553LVS00007B/88-114